The European Union

The European Union
A Critical Guide

Steven P. McGiffen

Pluto Press

LONDON • STERLING, VIRGINIA

First published 2001 by Pluto Press
345 Archway Road, London N6 5AA
and 22883 Quicksilver Drive,
Sterling, VA 20166–2012, USA

www.plutobooks.com

British Library Cataloguing in Publication Data
A catalogue record for this book is available from the British Library

Library of Congress Cataloging in Publication Data
McGiffen, Steven P., 1954–
    The European Union : a critical guide / Steven P. McGiffen.
        p. cm.
    ISBN 0–7453–1696–4 (hardback) — ISBN 0–7453–1695–6 (pbk.)
    1. European Union. 2. Political planning—European Union countries.
    I. Title.
    JN32 .M34 2001
    341.242'2—dc21
                                                                    2001002159

ISBN 0 7453 1696 4 hardback
ISBN 0 7453 1695 6 paperback

10	09	08	07	06	05	04	03	02	01
10	9	8	7	6	5	4	3	2	1

Designed and produced for Pluto Press by
Chase Publishing Services, Fortescue, Sidmouth EX10 9QG
Typeset from disk by Stanford DTP Services, Towcester
Printed in the European Union by TJ International, Padstow

Contents

Boxes

The European Union: An Uncritical Guide to the Abbreviations and Acronyms

ACP	Trade co-operation body comprising EU and developing countries
ASEAN	Association of South East Asian Nations
ASP	Agreement on Social Policy
CAP	Common Agricultural Policy
CCT	Common Customs Tariff
CEE	Central and Eastern Europe
CEEP	EU-wide small businesses' group
CFP	Common Fisheries Policy
CFSP	Common Foreign and Security Policy
CI	Community Initiative
CMO	Common Market Organisation (under the CAP)
Comett	EU education and training programme, now defunct
COREPER	Committee of Member States' Permanent Representatives
CP	Common Position (i.e. adopted by Council)
CPs	Community programmes
CTP	Common Transport Policy
DG	Directorate General (a division of the Commission)
EAGGF	European Agricultural Guidance and Guarantee Fund
EAP	Environmental Action Programme
EC	European Community
ECB	European Central Bank
ECHR	European Convention on Human Rights
ECJ	European Court of Justice
Ecofin	Economic and Finance Council
ECOSOC	Economic and Social Committee
ECSC	European Coal and Steel Community
ECU	European Currency Unit
EEA	European Economic Area
EEB	European Environmental Board
EFTA	European Free Trade Area

EIB	European Investment Bank
EIF	European Investment Fund
ELDR	Liberal group in the EP
EMS	European Monetary System
EMU	European Monetary Union
EP	European Parliament
Equal	Community Initiative to encourage equal opportunities
Erasmus	EU university education programme, now defunct
ERDF	European Regional Development Fund
ESCB	European System of Central Banks
ESF	European Social Fund
EU	European Union
EEC	European Economic Community
ETUC	European Trade Union Council
ETUI	European Trade Union Institute
Euratom	European Atomic Energy Community
Eures	European Employment Service
Europol	EU police force
EWC	European Works Council
FIFG	Financial Instrument for Fisheries Guidance
GATT	General Agreement on Tariffs and Trade
GDP	Gross Domestic Product
GSP	Generalised System of Preferences (under external trade rules)
GUE-NGL	Left group in the EP
Helios	EU-funded network for disabled people, now defunct
Horizon	Community Initiative to address unemployment, now defunct
IGC	Intergovernmental Conference
ILO	International Labour Organisation
IMF	International Monetary Fund
Inter-reg III	Community Initiative for border regions
ISPA	Structural fund for CEE applicant countries
JHA	Justice and Home Affairs
JRC	(EU) Joint Research Council
Leader	Community Initiative for poorer regions
Leonardo	EU training and education programme
LIFE	EU fund to support nature conservation projects
Lingua	EU language education programme, now defunct
Mercosur	Latin American economic community

MAGP	Multi-annual Guidance Programme (under CFP)
MNCs	Multinational Corporations
NAFTA	North American Free Trade Area
NATO	North Atlantic Treaty Organisation
NGO	Non-governmental organisation
NI	*Non-inscrit*: independent Member of EP
NOW	New Opportunities for Women – an employment initiative, now defunct
OECD	Organisation for Economic Co-operation and Development
PDB	Preliminary Draft Budget
PES	'Party of European Socialists': centre-left group in the EP
PHARE	Development programme for CEE applicant countries
PPE-ED	'European People's Party': the centre-right group in the EP
QMV	Qualified Majority Voting
R&D	Research and Development
SAFE	Small fund to support SMEs making health and safety improvements
SAP	Structural adjustment programme
SAPARD	Rural development fund for CEE applicant countries
SEA	Single European Act
SEM	Single European Market
SMEs	Small and Medium Sized Enterprises
SMUS	alternative term – 'U' is for Undertakings
Socrates	EU education programme
TAC	Total Allowable Catch (under the CFP)
TDI	A ragbag group in the EP including fascists and others
TENs	Trans European Networks
TEU	Treaty on European Union – the 'Maastricht Treaty'
UEN	Group of the Union for a Europe of Nations
UNCTAD	United Nations Council for Trade and Development
UNHCR	United Nations High Commission for Refugeess
UNICE	EU-wide employers' group
Urban	Community Initiative for urban regions
VAT	Value Added tax
WEU	Western European Union
WTO	World Trade Organisation

Preface
The European Union:
Books, Websites and Propaganda

At the back of this book you will find a list of recommended books, papers and websites which I hope you will find comprehensive and useful. The inclusion of so long a bibliography might well beg the question as to whether, if so much is already available, and written on such a wide range of EU-related subjects from so many points of view, the world really needs yet another book on the Union and its ways. After all, the material listed varies from general guides to Euro-federalist tracts, and from specialised scholarly treatises to diatribes against 'Brussels' and all its works.

Despite this wealth of literature, however, gaps remain, and it is the aim of this book to fill the biggest and most glaring of these. The fact is that, whilst people who already have some knowledge of the Union can easily find well-written books on particular subjects which come from a number of points of view, those students seeking to get to grips with what at first sight seems a dauntingly complex subject have no such choice. Almost every available book which describes, for the general reader or beginning student, the basic procedures by which the European Union is governed, is written from within a certain range of opinion. Each either celebrates or accepts as an immutable fact the current Union and its systems of governance and economic relations.

This does not mean that they are invariably propagandistic tracts or that they do not, in some cases, offer useful guides to their subject. On the contrary, books such as Dick Leonard's *Guide to the European Union,* Bainbridge and Teasdale's *Penguin Companion to the European Union* or John McCormick's *Understanding the European Union* will each give you the information you need to make sense of the EU. None, however, gives a thorough account of the range of criticisms of the Union found across Europe.

On the other hand, critical works rarely give much help to those seeking a basic introduction. An exception is the Institute of Directors publication, Roney and Budd's *The European Union: A Guide*

Through the EU/EC Maze, or the more up-to-date *EC/EU Fact Book*, by Alex Roney, though the first of these is aimed at business people rather than students or the general reader. Another is the on-line *Euroknow* encyclopaedia, which rivals a book like Rodney Leach's *Europe: A Concise Encylopaedia* and even manages to be amusing. These, however, are guides of a rather different kind to the one I set out to write. They are reference works more than critical essays. In *The European Union: A Critical Guide*, I have attempted to combine the two, giving as straightforward an account as possible of the sometimes labyrinthine bureaucracy, the treaties and the economic imperatives by which the Union is governed, before tackling questions such as the dilution of democracy or the influence of big corporations.

It is generally recognised that support for the European Union and its integrationist agenda comes from across the political spectrum. Some on the left have seen the EU as offering the potential, even if inadvertently, for generating closer and more effective cooperation between the labour movement or radical forces in different member states; others, left as well as right, argue that the Union has the potential to act as a counterweight to the overwhelming power of the United States. Even Fidel Castro expressed this idea when he welcomed the establishment of the Euro. Greens, at least outside the UK, Ireland and Scandinavia, have been overwhelmingly positive, extrapolating from the self-evident fact that many environmental problems demand an international solution, to an enthusiasm for a European federation. On the right, on the other hand, the EC/EU has garnered support on the basis of the Treaty of Rome's absolute commitment to a market economy, the clear advantages for corporate business to be found in the removal of barriers to trade across a huge 'internal' market, and the fact that each step of integration has made the sorts of policies traditionally favoured by governments to the left of centre difficult if not actually illegal.

Opposition to the EU also comes from many sources. This fact is, however, at least in the UK and, in my experience, North America, far less known. In the English-speaking world the so-called 'Euro-sceptic' or 'anti-European' position has been pigeon-holed as an atavistic right-wing set of beliefs which have grown in the main from a failure to accept the realities of the late twentieth, early twenty-first-century world, of globalisation and the irrelevance of the nation state to modern power politics.

In this view of politics we have, on the one side, forward-looking, internationally-minded, dynamic, go-ahead (and so on) leaders who have a 'vision of Europe' and wish to avoid any possibility of the return of the sort of national rivalry which generated an enmity that led in turn to several large wars in the nineteenth century and two huge ones in the twentieth. On the other we have the sort of people who wear Union Jack waistcoats and are concerned to defend every Englishman's God-given right to watch dogs tearing up small furry animals, to eat crisps containing flavourings considered poisonous elsewhere in the world, and to have a public transport system which would be the envy of remoter regions of Burma. Elsewhere in Europe, there is no opposition whatsoever, except in Scandinavia, which is supposed to be a bit odd anyway and where, no doubt, there are people who wear waistcoats displaying the Swedish or Danish or Scandinavian flag, and insist on their right to chew tobacco and do other, non-internationally-minded things which have no place in the globalised economy.

One of the aims of this book is to dispel this myth, which has been created by pro-EU propagandists but, it has to be said, eagerly embraced by the sort of Eurosceptic it describes, a type which does, unfortunately, exist. In my dealings with the anti-EU movement I have met young Danes who were convinced that the European Union was a sort of Soviet Union#2, and one who, despite what appeared to be extreme poverty, travelled to Brussels from Copenhagen by train rather than the cheaper bus because the bus company was called Eurolines and he refused to use it – though it is just possible that he was joking. I have seen it argued, quite seriously, that the English common law and the legal system based upon it are inherently fairer than those based on Roman law and the Napoleonic code. (Tell that to the Birmingham Six.) And I have heard the EU blamed for such phenomena as the pitiful level of pensions in the UK, over-lenient treatment of child molesters, and global warming.

On the other hand, I have met elected British politicians who express breathless enthusiasm for 'Europe' only because it is fashionable to do so, yet know nothing whatsoever about what the EU can and cannot do and can speak not a word of any language other than what now passes for English in parliamentary circles; I have met politicians and journalists from across Europe who understand very little about the relationship between the EU and its member states; I met, quite recently, an environmentalist campaigner and journalist who was unable even to guess why some people believe that the Union and its predecessors have done far more harm to the environment than good. Ignorance of the EU is not confined to those who oppose or criticise it.

The subtext of much of what is written on the subject, and of absolutely all official material issued by the European Commission or the European Parliament, is that criticism is not a useful activity. It is not the job of the citizenry to call into question the existence or nature of this Union. We may criticise its policy, but not the thing itself. Thus, much of the material listed in the bibliographies of the first four chapters of this work – before we begin to get down to details of particular policy areas – sets out not to discuss whether the Treaties of Rome, Maastricht, Amsterdam and Nice offer the best, or even a workable, solution to the problems facing the 15 member states and their peoples. It merely describes what is, and if it criticises at all it does so from the point of view which I have called *integrationism* – more often, though misleadingly, referred to as *federalism* – a belief that integration has not gone nearly far enough, that it is stalled by narrow national self-interest, that it is, or will be, 'the Future'. This does not mean it is worthless: on the contrary, much of this material – a prime example of which would be Nicholas Mussis' *Handbook of the European Union* – is meticulously researched and clearly written, if a bit short on humour. It should not, however, be taken at face value. These people have a clear political agenda, as clear as that of the anti-EU movement, and their books should be read with this in mind.

There are exceptions, of course, and not merely in Martin Holmes' 1996 collection *The Eurosceptic Reader*. The 'euro-know' on-line encyclopedia of the EU (at http://www.euro-know.org/dictionary/e.html) is one of the few attempts by critics of the Union really to get to grips with how it works, and it is both useful and entertaining. Daniel Guégen's *Practical Guide to the EU Labyrinth*, though the translation from the original French could be improved, is the most straightforward, least ideological, simple description, with useful diagrams, of the workings of the Union's various institutions and the relationships between them. A good book for cramming, used in conjunction with the range of official websites given in the bibliography or accessible through the European Parliament's home page at http://www.europarl.eu.int/home/, it will tell you all you need to know about the EU's structure and processes, unless you wish to read a discussion of whether, how or why these are undermining democracy, removing decision-making from a level accessible to the people, or facilitating the growing power of big corporations.

As well as 'guides' to the EU, academic studies of the Union or aspects of it are common, though again, those which take an anti-integrationist line or draw conclusions which call the basic tenets of the Treaty of Rome into question are few. To find intelligent criticism it is better to look at studies of particular policies or policy areas or developments, both academic and those written for a wider audience. Swedish Green Euro-MP Per Gahrton provided the best analysis of the Amsterdam Treaty from an oppositional viewpoint with his *The New EU After Amsterdam*. Gahrton is good on the Common Foreign and Security Policy, as is his Green colleague, Irish MEP Patricia McKenna, whose analysis of Amsterdam can be read on line (the URL is given in the bibliography of Chapter 6). Michael Spencer's *States of Injustice* is a critical study of the policy areas covered by the Justice and Home Affairs section of that treaty. Andor and Summers' *Market Failure*, though its subject is broader, is essential background reading for anyone who wants to understand what lies behind the EU's curious stop–go attitude to its own enlargement eastwards.

The Euro has of course provoked passionate comment from all sides, with Bernard H. Moss's *The Single European Currency in National Perspective: A Community in Crisis* being an excellent, and relatively recent oppositional study which is detailed but accessible. I have been unable to find anything of this quality when it comes to the single internal market, and so have attempted, in Chapter 9, to explain in as much detail as space would allow why this concept lies at the heart of the integrationist project and why it is, in my view, incompatible with any political programme which would, before the advent of Blairism transformed the meaning of the word, have been recognised as having anything to do with the left.

External relations should provide fertile ground for anyone wishing to demonstrate that the EU is no internationalist project. In general, however, the Union tends to be given an easy ride by critics of globalisation. Oxfam UK's website, for example (see bibliography for Chapter 10) is critical, but the title of its statement on the subject, *The European Union: A Potential Global Force for Change*, demonstrates the limitations of its criticisms. It is hard to imagine a development NGO publishing something called *The World Trade Organisation: A Potential Global Force for Change*. Yet the EU and WTO work on the basis of precisely the same economic philosophy and undermine popular democracy in much the same ways.

Employment and unemployment have been the subject of much attention during the last quarter century, since mass joblessness returned to plague developed economies. Valerie Symes *Unemployment and Employment Policy in the European Union* is a comprehensive discussion of the issue. Once again, however, most criticism accepts the EU and its right to have competence in this area, and does not question the official line, which is that unemployment is a product of market dysfunction rather than an essential feature of a capitalist economy. This heresy has now been buried under a division of opinion which would have been seen as hopelessly narrow at any time before the mid-'80s: between those who see the solution as extensive deregulation and the dismantling of the welfare state, and those who see the solution as less extensive deregulation and the dismantling of parts of the welfare state. A sort of neo-Keynesian thought remains influential within the European Commission and some member-state governments, but unlike Keynesianism proper it involves no fundamental analysis of what makes capitalism work.

The environment has produced a much more impressive body of criticism of the EU and its policies, which, when agriculture and transport are added to the equation, have been largely responsible for the destruction of the Western European countryside over the last almost half a century. Wyn Grant's work on the environment and farming policies and their inter-relationship and effects is outstandingly good. The best sources of critical comment, however, are the website and publications of the European Environmental Bureau (EEB), a body which brings together a wide range of environmental NGOs.

Transport has also provoked some of the most intelligent and informed critiques of EU policies, as well as the broader context of global and regional developments towards ever-less sustainable transport systems. This can be found, *inter alia*, in the books of John Whitelegg, which have the thoroughness which one should expect from an academic approach whilst also being exceptionally readable. Winfried Wolf's *Car Mania* contains some useful comment on EU transport policies. Once you've decided that they have to be opposed, however, you really need to get hold of the green activist group A SEED Europe's *Lost in Concrete,* subtitled *Activist Guide to European Transport Policies.*

Other areas of policy really need the kind of radical critical attention given to the environment, transport, agriculture, trade and development, and to a lesser extent to employment and social policy. Even on line, it is hard to find more than a narrow range of views on such subjects as industrial or competition policy. Right-wing 'euro-sceptics' have their websites and comment on every aspect of their enemy's ways, but much of this is ill-informed.

Of course, the nature of the Internet, its constant rapid growth, and even the volume of conventional literature which appears each year mean that these gaps may well be filled. This book attempts to give an idea of the range of possible criticism, to question the EU at a more fundamental level than is usually seen, and thus to contribute directly to this flow of information.

1 Introduction

'Criticism of the European Union is akin to blasphemy and could be restricted without violating freedom of speech' – Advocate-General at the European Court of Justice (in case C-274/99)

In 1957 six countries of Western Europe signed a treaty designed to further the transformation of the economic and political life of the region. The act of signing itself demonstrated that much had changed in the twelve years since the end of World War Two. In 1945, most of Western Europe had been in ruins.

Though the aims of the Treaty of Rome were always as much political as economic, it originally limited the Community's powers to matters concerned with production and consumption. The Six jealously guarded their control of taxation, of the criminal law, of moral and cultural matters, of education. Their co-operation was, ostensibly at least, designed to pool economic resources and resourcefulness, not to dissolve Western Europe into a single amorphous entity.

Whether the European Union descended from this original Community should be an economic tool or a fully-fledged federation is now the tension at the heart of the continent's politics. Important decisions are involved, and the future of every country in Europe will depend on their outcome. They are inherently difficult, but are made even more so for British people by the bizarre terms in which the debate is almost invariably conducted in UK political life and in the country's media. Commonly used expressions such as 'pro-European', 'anti-European' and 'Eurosceptic' are deliberately misleading, and the equation of 'Europe' with the European Union both geographically and politically inaccurate. Much comment, moreover, on all sides of the debate, is ill-informed about the basics of the system.

The European Union is a political and economic project which a number of governments have decided to pursue. It is not an inevitable outcome of some mysterious March of History, nor is it a boat or train which must under no circumstances be missed. Politicians who abandon reasoned argument in favour of muddy metaphors (which, for some reason, almost always involve modes

1

of transport) generally do so because they are lying. To be for or against the European Union, to favour its deepening into a full political union, its complete disbanding or something between the two, has nothing at all to do with patriotism.

The EU is a proposed answer to the problems of Britain, Ireland and their neighbours on the European mainland. It is not the only available answer and it may not be the best, but it is quite possible to support or oppose it with the best of intentions. To fly the twelve-star flag is not an act of treason, to refuse to do so no retreat into xenophobia. The EU exists, and the people of its member states must decide what they want to do about that fact. In this book, which may be the first introduction to the subject written by someone – to put my own cards on the table – with deep doubts about the Union in anything like its present form, I shall attempt to provide the reader with the information he or she needs to be able to take part in that historic decision.

2   The Treaties

Before the mid-1980s, changes to the Treaty of Rome were relatively rare. Some amendments were necessary when new states joined, and two treaties were signed, coming into force in 1971 and 1977 respectively, dealing with budgetary matters.

It was in 1987, however, with the signing of the so-called Single European Act (SEA), that things began to move at such a pace that the Act can, in retrospect, be seen as the beginning of a transformation of the European Economic Community into the European Union. At first sight, the SEA seems well in keeping with a notion of the EEC as 'the Common Market'. The central thrust was a commitment by the member states to remove all remaining barriers to trade. 'Barriers to trade' can, however, be a very inclusive term, and the implications of a drive to remove them reached into every corner of economic life.

The SEA gave the member states until the last day of 1992 to achieve an 'internal market' within which the movement of goods, services, capital and labour would be unrestricted.

The Act did not, moreover, limit itself entirely to trade issues. It adopted also a series of institutional reforms aimed at improving co-operation between heads of state and government and attempted to take some steps towards achieving the important integrationist goal of a common foreign and defence policy. In addition, it extended Community competence[1] into new fields which would become of huge importance in the following decade: social policy, environmental protection, and research and development.

MAASTRICHT

Before 1992 the pretty Dutch border town of Maastricht was known mainly for its pleasant cafés and annual antiques fair. The signing of the Treaty on European Union on 7 February of that year changed all that, and the name 'Maastricht' became, overnight, synonymous with the first really major overhaul of the Treaty of Rome.

Maastricht did four things which were of transforming significance for the integrationist project. Firstly, like the Single European

3

Act, it extended the competence of the Community's institutions into new areas. Secondly, it established new and far-reaching objectives which were openly integrationist[2] in character. Thirdly, it aimed to create a single currency, wrote a timetable for its introduction and set out the rules by which member states would qualify for admission and by which the currency would be governed. Finally, the SEA created a wholly new structure within which the European Community would be one of three 'pillars' propping up the European Union, the other two being the Common Foreign and Security Policy (CFSP) and Justice and Home Affairs (JHA).

Of the three pillars, one, the European Community, is much more important as a support for the edifice of European Union than are the other two. The Community itself can be seen as constituting a number of different sets of institutions and practices.

The first is an internal market without barriers to trade, a concept which includes, but is more far-reaching than, a simple customs union. In a customs union, independent nations agree not to put tariffs on each others' goods. The internal market carries this further, however, following a rigorous logic: if one country cannot impose tariffs on imports from another, goes the logic, then it is entitled to ask whether those goods are produced, and traded, under conditions which ensure fair competition. Moreover, the internal market is more than a simple customs union in that it does not simply guarantee the free movement of goods, but what have been called *the four freedoms*: free movement of goods, capital, services and labour. Each of these 'freedoms' also carries with it far-reaching implications which compromise each member state's ability to run its own affairs.

The Economic and Monetary Union (EMU) is the second major element of Maastricht's revamped European Community. The Treaty contains not a vague, hopeful commitment to the eventual introduction of a single currency, but a detailed plan for a union of economies presided over by a common central bank.

The creation of Maastricht's other two pillars was made necessary by the continuing struggle between integrationists and those who felt that the process of transfer of powers from national to supranational institutions had gone far enough. Both foreign policy and the criminal law, two of the major elements, respectively, of the second pillar, Common Foreign and Security Policy (CFSP) and the third, Justice and Home Affairs (JHA), are matters traditionally regarded as fundamental to sovereignty, or the right and ability of an independent state to govern its own affairs and those of the inhabitants of its territory. For this reason they were kept outside the normal supra-national structures of the European Community.

As well as leaving us with an extremely complex structure, the tension between integrationists and their opponents was resolved in another way at Maastricht, by underlining a concept which had been around for some time in EC circles, but which had never before been institutionalised: 'subsidiarity'. Though this is not always the case in practice, on paper subsidiarity is simple. Applied to the EU, it implies that its institutions can take action only where the objectives of such action could not be achieved at the national level. In addition, proposed measures are supposed to display 'proportionality', meaning that they must not be any stronger, more far-reaching or more expensive than is justified by the seriousness of the problem they address.

AMSTERDAM

Given its other attractions, Amsterdam is unlikely ever to see its name reduced to a shorthand label for a Treaty, despite that Treaty's importance for the political direction of the European Union and its neighbours. Though Amsterdam did not introduce anything so obviously transforming as a currency union, it did take the European Union further down the road towards becoming, if not precisely a supra-national state, something very much more than a set of institutions to facilitate co-operation between independent nations. In the official view, the Amsterdam Treaty was an attempt 'to create the political and institutional conditions to enable the European Union to meet the challenges of the future ... the rapid evolution of the international situation, the globalisation of the economy and its impact on jobs, the fight against terrorism, international crime and drug trafficking, ecological problems and threats to public health'.[3] On the other hand, Irish Green Euro-MP Patricia McKenna has described it as 'a further step towards Fortress Europe' which signals 'clear moves towards a militarised European Union'. Social policy innovations are, McKenna said, 'window-dressing and lip-service'.[4]

NICE

The Treaty signed at Nice in February, 2001 was supposed to deal with what were referred to as the Amsterdam 'leftovers': the weighting of votes under Qualified Majority Voting (QMV) and how many would constitute an effective majority or a blocking minority; representation in the European Parliament; the size and powers of the Commission; and the whole question of the EU's institutions and the relationship amongst them and between each and the member states. In the event, a number of additional unresolved issues were on the Nice table: the Charter of Fundamental Rights, the question of allowing groups of countries to go further along the path of integration than the rest were prepared to do; possible rein-forcement of the Common Foreign and Security Policy.

Despite this intimidating agenda, Nice turned out to be much less sweeping in the changes it introduced to the structure of the Union than were the transforming agreements at Maastricht and Amsterdam. It was, however, even more confusing than either of those labyrinthine texts, with the governments of member states and applicant countries haggling for months afterwards about the exact meaning of various articles. Even the facts of the matter were a subject of dispute, whilst the question of the weighting of votes at Council and the number of members of the European Parliament a country would have, and whether everyone would get a place on the Commission, were fudged.

There was, nevertheless, a sort of consensus regarding the political significance of the Treaty. Integrationists saw it as a botched agreement with a few saving graces; opponents and critics of the EU mirrored this, in general drawing attention to what they saw as certain dangerous features whilst conceding that it might have been worse. Some powers were transferred from national institutions to Brussels; QMV was extended to several new areas, but fewer than was hoped/feared; the weighting of votes was favourable to the big countries, but less so than it might have been; small countries kept their right to a Commissioner, but only for the time being.

Once again, a Treaty embodied the tension at the heart of a Union moving cautiously towards a form of integration about which many politicians across the spectrum harboured grave doubts and which had extremely limited popular support. Nice was supposed to facilitate enlargement, but if it did so it was in a way whose benefits for multinational corporations and political elites were clear, and clearly gained at the cost of a further reduction in the power and influence of the peoples of the member states and their elected representatives.

Notwithstanding the reforms agreed at Nice, it continues to be the major revisions of Maastricht and Amsterdam which determine the direction of the European Union. All three Treaties dealt with a wide variety of policy areas including asylum and immigration, freedom of movement, citizenship, employment, social policy, discrimination, the environment and public health, consumer protection, open government, and foreign policy, including defence. Finally, it introduced certain reforms to the way the Union's institutions conduct business. These innovations are best discussed in the light of developments and each major policy area, as well as the institutions which govern the Union, are covered in later chapters.

Box 2.1

Major Provisions of the Single European Act (1987)

- Added six new policy areas to European Community competence: single market, monetary co-operation, social policy, cohesion (i.e. between richer and poorer regions), research and development, environmental standards.
- Extended European Parliament's powers: Council of Ministers could overrule EP veto in most policy areas pertaining to the single market only by a unanimous vote.
- Introduced qualified majority voting (QMV) in the Council, ending the national veto in most areas pertaining to the single market.
- Gave formal standing to the European Council, by which the heads of state and government of the member states meet to discuss and determine policy.
- Declared that the single internal EC market would be completed by December 1992 and all remaining barriers to intra-Community trade removed.

(The full text of the SEA can be found at http://europa.eu.int/abc/obj/treaties/en/entr14a.h)

Box 2.2

Major Provisions of the Treaty on European Union (TEU) – the 'Maastricht Treaty', Signed December 1991

- Establishment of the European Union (EU) with a three-pillar structure:

1. The European Community (EC)
2. Common foreign and security policy (CFSP)
3. Justice and home affairs co-operation (JHA).

CFSP and JHA are 'intergovernmental':

– they cannot issue Directives and Regulations (EC laws)
– they are conducted by national governments through the Council of Ministers and the European Council
– they give no formal powers to the supranational institutions – the Commission, EP and European Court of Justice (ECJ).

- Establishment of a timetable and conditions for economic and monetary union (EMU), including a single currency.
- Establishment of European Union citizenship.
- Further extension of EC competence: to education, culture, 'trans-European networks'; extension of existing powers in environmental policy, industrial policy and R&D expanded.
- Agreement by eleven member states (excluding UK) on Social Chapter.
- Further extension of powers of EP.
- Establishment of Cohesion Fund.
- ECJ given power to levy fines on member states.
- Subsidiarity written into text of Treaty.
- Introduction of a Common Foreign and Security Policy (CFSP, the Second Pillar) with limited provision for QMV and a statement of intent to build a common defence.
- Introduction of powers related to Justice and Home Affairs (JHA, the Third Pillar) and dealing with such matters as asylum policy and policing

Box 2.3

Major Provisions of the Amsterdam Treaty (1997)

Extension of Qualified Majority Voting

- Extends QMV to the following fields: employment guidelines and incentive measures; social exclusion; free movement of persons (after five years); special treatment for foreign nationals; public health; equal opportunities and equal treatment for men and women; research and development; countering fraud; customs co-operation; statistics; data protection; peripheral regions.

Institutional Changes

- Limits the number of members of the European Parliament to 700, however big the EU may grow.
- Nomination of Commission President by member states must be approved by Parliament; the Members of the Commission are to be nominated by common accord between the governments and the President; President to define the Commission's general political guidelines.
- ECJ given direct responsibility for ensuring that human rights are respected and its jurisdiction extended to the fields of immigration, asylum, visas and the crossing of borders, and police and judicial and criminal co-operation.
- EU Court of Auditors given new investigative powers.

Development of CFSP

- Provides for greater co-operation between member states in pursuit of a Common Foreign and Security Policy.
- Empowers the Union to carry out humanitarian aid and peace-keeping tasks (known as Petersberg tasks), to devise common strategies, general foreign policy guidelines, joint actions and common positions.
- The EU to be represented by a group (called the *troika*) consisting of the Presidency of the Council, the Commission and the Secretary-General of the Council, who will act as the Union's 'High Representative for the common foreign and security policy' (a new post).

Social Questions and Civil Rights

- Empowers the Council to take appropriate action to combat discrimination based on sex, racial or ethnic origin, religion or belief, disability, age or sexual orientation and provides measures to combat discrimination based on disability. Makes the furtherance of gender equality a Community task.
- Provides for permanent and regular collaboration, within the Community framework, on employment and unemployment.

- Protects individuals from the processing of personal data and the free movement of such information by institutions and administrations that handle it.

Internal Security

- Provides for closer co-operation between police forces and customs authorities and directly with Europol, the European police network.
- Establishes a legal requirement to have closer co-operation between member states' police and judicial authorities to combat and prevent racism, xenophobia, terrorism, organised crime, trafficking of persons and offences against children, drug trafficking, corruption and fraud.
- Establishes a common minimum standard for rules, and penalties for organised crime, terrorism and drug trafficking will be adopted across the European Union.

Inward Migration

- Incorporates the Schengen agreement, providing for an area without impediment to free movement of travel between 13 of the 15 member states (UK and Denmark excluded), into the Treaty previously an intergovernmental accord, but also provides for the removal of all controls on people crossing internal borders – whether EU citizens or nationals of non-member countries ; in respect of controls at all the European Union's external borders, the establishment of common standards and procedures for checking people, common rules on visas for intended stays of no more than three months, a common list of non-member countries whose nationals must hold visas when crossing external borders, and a list of non-member countries whose nationals are exempt from this requirement, common procedures and conditions for the issue of visas by member states, and a definition of the terms on which nationals of non-member countries shall be free to travel within the EU for three months (it should be emphasised that the Treaty obliged the member states to develop these; it did not draw them up).
- Defines minimum standards for the reception of asylum seekers in member states, and for classifying nationals of non-member countries as refugees.

- Lays down the terms of entry and residence of immigrants in the European Union, and standards for procedures for the issue of long-term visas and residence permits by member states, standards for dealing with illegal immigration and illegal residence, and the repatriation of illegal residents, and the rights of citizens of non-member countries who are legally resident in a member state and the terms on which they may reside in other member states.

The Environment, Public Health and Consumer Protection

- Stipulates that a high level of human health protection must be assured in the definition and implementation of all Community policies and activities.
- Provides for a high level of consumer protection.

Environment must be taken into account in all Community policies. Commission obliged to conduct an environmental impact assessment of its own proposals. Environment, public health and consumer protection legislation now covered (with rare exceptions) by the co-decision procedure, giving the European Parliament some power over these areas.

For the full text of both Maastricht and Amsterdam Treaties go to http://www.fletcher.tufts.edu/multi/texts/eucons.txt

Box 2.4

Major Provisions of the Treaty of Nice, Signed February 2001

New Protocol on Enlargement adopted.
  QMV extended to new areas, principally:

- certain high-level appointments, including the President of the Commission and the High Representative for the Common Foreign and Security Policy;
- certain aspects of the making of international agreements;
- actions taken in support of anti-discrimination measures adopted by the member states;
- certain actions taken to enable citizens to take advantage of freedom of movement;

- most measures related to visas, asylum and immigration;
- granting of emergency financial assistance to member states;
- most industrial policy measures;
- from 2007, or the date of the adoption of the financial perspective for 2007–13 if no agreement has been reached before 2007, measures relating to the Structural Funds;
- financial and technical co-operation agreements with third countries (does not apply to association agreements or pre-accession measures).

Formalisation of 'Enhanced Co-operation' – groups of at least eight member states may make agreements among themselves which enable them to go further in particular policy areas than the rest are prepared to do, provided such agreements:

- further the objectives of the EU and reinforce integration;
- respect the Treaties and the single institutional framework of the Union;
- respect existing EU law;
- respect existing competences;
- do not undermine the internal market or economic and social cohesion;
- respects the competences, rights and obligations of non-participating member states;
- are in principle open to all member states;
- are used only as a last resort.

New judicial co-operation body, Eurojust, established.

Clear procedure for amending the fundamental aims of the Union, in consultation with the ECB and by unanimous vote at Council.

Commission President given more power to manage the Commission, and to force the resignation of an individual Commissioner. From 2005, Commission to consist of one member per member state until membership of the EU reaches 27. After that, membership to be fixed at a number, and according to a system of national rotation, to be determined by unanimous vote at Council.

Maximum number of Members of the European Parliament fixed at 732.

Establishment of an advisory Social Protection Committee.

Procedure defined for setting up 'political parties at European level'.

Some European Council meetings (which currently take place in the country holding the Presidency) to be held in Brussels. From the accession of the 18th member state, all European Council meetings to be held in Brussels.

The Conclusions of the Presidency of the European Council meeting at which the new Treaty was agreed can be found at http://www.europarl.eu.int/summits/nice1_en.htm#II. The Treaty itself can be found at http://www.europarl.eu.int/

3   The Institutions

At its current stage of development, the European Union is a curious amalgam of two things. Firstly, it remains to some extent a system to facilitate co-operation between independent member states, each of which has control over its own foreign policy, criminal law and, with certain limited but important exceptions, taxation. Secondly, however, it has in other areas evolved true supra-national institutions which have powers quite independently of the member states, including, in some cases, the right to instruct and discipline those member states. The future development of the EU will depend upon which of these gets the upper hand.

The current governing institutions reflect this state of flux. Some involve direct representation of member state governments, whilst others are entirely supra-national in nature. The most important of the former in terms of power is the European Council. As far as daily decision-making is concerned, however, it is the Council of Ministers.

THE EUROPEAN COUNCIL

The European Council brings together the heads of government of each of the EU's member states for regular, formal meetings at which decisions are taken which determine the immediate and longer-term direction of the Union. European Council meetings are attended by each country's prime minister and minister of foreign affairs, as well as the President of the European Commission and one of his Vice-Presidents. They have generally taken place in the Presidency country, but this is about to change following a decision taken at Nice and included in the new Treaty. From 2002, half of the European Council meetings will take place in Brussels; from the admission of the 18th member state, they will all be held there. This is clearly a question of practicalities and security, as well as a response to the amount of money host countries tend to spend on the show, but it seems an odd move for a body which, by its own admission, is seen as too remote from the people.

The European Council's task is, firstly, to discuss any business which cannot be dealt with in any other way, usually because no provision exists for it in the Treaties or because there is a known difference of opinion between member states as to whether such provision does exist, over what is known as the interpretation of the Treaties. However much care is taken with the wording of a treaty, or of any measure taken by the European Union, whether and how it is applied in a concrete situation may sometimes be open to debate. Ultimately, the Court of Justice decides such disputes. The European Council, however, represents in part an attempt to keep them out of court by bringing together the highest authority in each member state government to broker compromise agreements.

Secondly, the European Council takes often far-reaching decisions over the Union's direction. These will sometimes demand a change in the Treaty or, short of that, a new Community measure, a Directive or Regulation, which will then have to be formally proposed by the Commission before being approved by the member states and, in most cases, the European Parliament.

Finally, the European Council allows government leaders simply to chat, to air their views to each other on a range of topics, in a relatively informal milieu. This is no doubt pleasant for them, but more importantly it can provide an early warning system for potential problems and allow opinions to be sounded out. What precisely goes on in the palatial and usually secluded surroundings which are invariably chosen as the venue for these gatherings is, however, a matter for conjecture. In common with the other major decision-making bodies of the European Union – with the exception of the European Parliament – the European Council shrouds itself in a Kremlin-like secrecy which seems to many quite out of keeping with what might be expected from a community of democratic nations.

THE COUNCIL OF THE EUROPEAN UNION, OR COUNCIL OF MINISTERS

The word 'council' is so beloved in EU circles that it has been used – as if there were not already sufficient potential for confusion – to mean two quite different bodies. Though the European Council, described above, brings together the most powerful governmental politicians, it is the Council of the European Union, known generally as the Council of Ministers or simply the Council, which takes decisions in particular policy areas.

Most people would naturally think of the European Parliament as the EU's legislature. In fact, however, the Parliament's powers, though they have grown with each Treaty revision, remain quite limited. It does have a legislative role, but only as junior partner to the Council of Ministers.

The Council is in reality not one single body but rather an abstract term covering several distinct fora. Each of these deals with one policy area and brings together the relevant minister or ministers from each member state. There is thus an Agriculture Council, an Environment Council, a Social Affairs Council and so on. In addition, the General Affairs Council is made up of foreign ministers, who may be accompanied by specialised ministers for European or EU affairs. Its task is to pull together decisions made by the separate 'Councils' and to deal with relations with third countries.

The Council Presidency

Each member state holds the Presidency for six months in a system of rotation based partly on the alphabet, and partly on an attempt to avoid two major countries or too many smaller countries holding it in succession. The Presidency's formal task is for its ministers to take the chair in meetings of the Council, which normally take place in the Presidency country, as do meetings of the European Council. There is, however, also an expectation that the member state in question will exercise a temporary and limited form of leadership over the rest, seeking to bring important items on to the agenda or re-invigorate proposals which, for one reason or another, have gone dormant. In chairing Council meetings, the minister from the President country has a formal responsibility to seek common ground between member states whose opinions differ, suggesting compromises.

At the beginning of its six-month term each holder of the Presidency publishes a programme of priorities for legislative action, which usually includes some measure which has been held up for years because no agreement has been found which can unblock it. Sometimes a Presidency will be able to claim a number of successes based on a comparison of this programme with what has actually been achieved when the six months are up. More often, the programme will turn out to have been little more than a wish list.

In addition, the Presidency organises a series of conferences, seminars and other events to which Euro-MPs, Commissioners and their staff, national parliamentarians and others are invited to discuss what are seen as the burning issues of the day. Finally, each country takes the opportunity of its Presidency to promote its culture, often by financing visits to Brussels, or tours of the rest of the Union, by artists, writers, theatre groups and so on. Because it does tend to put them in the spotlight, as well as entailing huge amounts of work for everyone from Cabinet First Secretaries to bar staff, the Presidency tends to be taken quite seriously by the member states. Smaller countries, in particular, are often at pains to show that they are quite capable of hosting the party.

COREPER

Although elected politicians make up the EU's two legislative bodies, civil servants naturally play a major role in the day-to-day running of the Union. The Council is served by the Committee of the Permanent Representatives of the Member States, known by its French acronym COREPER. COREPER prepares the agenda of Council meetings and then carries out its orders. If the Council has to examine a proposal from the Commission, it is usually COREPER which takes the first look. COREPER, like the Council itself, is a secretive body whose influence is extensive.

INTERGOVERNMENTAL CONFERENCES

Each revision of the Treaty has been preceded (and must be preceded) by an Intergovernmental conference (IGC). The Amsterdam IGC, which completed a decade of EC/EU reform, was the fourth in only eleven years, whereas only two had been held in the previous history of integration, since that which accompanied the establishment of the European Coal and Steel Community, the EC/EU's forerunner. The Amsterdam Treaty provided that, at least one year before the Union has more than 20 member states, a new intergovernmental conference must be convened. In fact, unanswered questions regarding enlargement led to the establishment of an IGC in 2000, resulting in a new Treaty, the Treaty of Nice. The Treaty of Nice in turn calls for a further IGC to begin in 2004.

THE COMMISSION OF THE EUROPEAN COMMUNITIES

Like COREPER, the European Commission (as it is invariably known) is made up of unelected men and women. Unlike COREPER, however, it has extensive formal powers.

From its inception in 1967, the Commission has grown in size with each enlargement of the Community. Since the admission of Finland, Austria and Sweden brought the number of EU states to 15, the Commission has had 20 members, with one each coming from the ten smaller countries and two from, respectively, Spain, Italy, Germany, Britain and France.

As in a conventional government, each member is given responsibility for a particular policy area or areas. The Commissioners are appointed by the member state governments, but are constitutionally independent of them. In other words, they may not take any form of instruction and are supposed to represent the interests of the European Community and make sure the Treaties are respected.

At Nice, the Commission President gained new powers. The President can now take decisions on the Commission's internal organisation 'in order to ensure that it acts consistently, efficiently and on the basis of collective responsibility'. Importantly, Commissioners can now be sacked by the President; or rather, like football managers, they can be forced to resign.

The Commission is the real driving force behind the integrationist project. It has two practical functions, both of which in practice give it immense power. Firstly, it proposes new laws and other measures. Though these are often done at the behest of the Council, and must then be approved (and can be amended) by the Council and in some cases by the Parliament as well, the fact that the Commission works on the detail of initial proposals gives it a decisive influence over policy.

Secondly, it is responsible for the day-to-day running of Community affairs, acting as a sort of hands-on executive with specific powers independent of the member states and laid down in the Treaties.

Thirdly, it is charged with ensuring that those same Treaties are correctly implemented and respected. In its own view it 'represents the common interest' standing above the national interests of the constituent parts of the Union, and its members are required to swear an oath to that effect.

The Commission President is appointed by the Council for a five-year term. In 'common accord' with the Council, he or she then chooses the rest of the Commission, and their appointees, together with the Presidential nominee, must then be approved *en bloc* by the European Parliament, which can also sack them – again only *en bloc* – at any time. However, this power, which at first glance appears to answer those critics who say that a Union run by appointees is hardly democratic, is less useful than it might seem.

What undermines it is the sheer finality of the sole measure at the disposal of the Parliament. All that the EP can do is sack (or refuse to accept the appointment of) the entire Commission *en bloc*. It cannot mete out any less drastic disciplinary measures, nor can it sack or refuse an individual Commissioner.

Many people believed that, because of the draconian nature of its only disciplinary power, the Parliament would never take the step of throwing a Commission out. This impression has been confirmed more than once when the EP, making itself look rather foolish in the process, has threatened to do just that before backing down at the last minute.

Such a view was, however, dealt a blow in March 1999 when the European Commission resigned in order to avoid the indignity of being fired, a fate which was beginning to seem increasingly likely. Of course, whether the Parliament would have gone through with its threat we will never know. Also, the peculiar circumstances surrounding the event must be acknowledged. Members of the European Parliament would have to stand for re-election only three months later, and poll returns were revealing the embarrassing fact that fewer than half of the eligible voters in the member states were intending to vote. It would be unfair, perhaps, to dismiss the whole event as a pre-election publicity stunt, but there was certainly at least an element of attention-seeking in the Parliament's behaviour. More importantly, however, the Santer Commission was mired in incompetence and corruption. Santer's undignified, blustering reaction to Parliament's allegations and his utter lack of apology for having appointed such inappropriate people to run 'Europe', were less than impressive.

Widespread corruption at the Commission had been revealed by the actions of one courageous employee, Paul van Buitenen. Early in December 1998 van Buitenen, an assistant auditor in the Financial Control Directorate, went public with a long list of financial irregularities that demonstrated what anyone who has dealings with the

Commission can see very well, that the institution is riddled with an elitist, anti-democratic ethos. The defensive reaction to van Buitenen's revelations, the open victimisation of the man who had made them, and the clear failure to understand what all the fuss was about, confirmed the truth of this impression. Here was a body which was not only corrupt but which exhibited the same kind of *esprit de corps* shown by certain police forces and military units, a sort of schoolboy code of silence which would be hilarious were it not so dangerous to the democratic process. Funds had disappeared, contracts had been awarded in extremely suspect circumstances, and numerous examples were uncovered, going to the very top of the institution, of what the Dutchman van Buitenen would term *vriend-jespolitiek* (literally, boyfriend/girlfriend politics) – and yet he was reviled by colleagues and victimised by his bosses for exposing these facts to the European Parliament. To its credit, whatever the mix of motives, the Parliament for once sounded credible when it threatened to act.

THE EUROPEAN PARLIAMENT

Until 1979, Members of the European Parliament were appointed by national parliaments from amongst their own members. Although this may sound less democratic, opponents of the EU in its present form argue that, controlled by national parliamentarians, the European Assembly, as it was often called in Britain, provided a truer and more effective counterbalance to the Council of Ministers. The introduction of direct elections was a victory for integrationists, and every addition to the powers of the European Parliament since then must be viewed in this light.

As with the Commission, the number of Members of the European Parliament has increased with each enlargement, with the entry of Sweden, Finland and Austria in 1997 bringing it to 626. At Nice in December 2000, the decision was taken to limit the number of members to 732, no matter how large the Union grows. Although this is a practical measure, it could also have a dramatic effect on the Parliament's composition, effectively raising the threshold a party needs to cross before it wins election. The result will be that the EP will come to be, even more so than at present, dominated by the two blocs of Social Democrats (organised as the Party of European Socialists), and Christian Democrats and other centre-right parties

Table 3.1 Membership of the European Parliament, 1999–2004

	B	D	Ger	Gr	Sp	Fr	Ire	I	L	N	A	P	Fin	Sw	UK	Total
PPE-DE	6	1	53	9	28	21	5	34	2	9	7	9	5	7	36	232
PES	5	3	35	9	24	22	1	16	2	6	7	12	3	6	30	181
ELDR	5	6			3		1	8	1	8			5	4	11	52
Greens/EFA	7		5		4	9	2	2	1	4	2		2	2	6	46
GUE/NGL		1	6	7	4	11		6		1		2	1	3		42
UEN		1				12	6	9				2				30
TDI	2					5		12								19
EDD		4				6				3					3	16
NI					1	1					5				1	8
Total	25	16	99	25	64	87	15	87	6	31	21	25	16	22	87	626

626 Members – situation as at 20 December 2000

Read across for member states, and down for political groups, which are as follows:

EPP – ED: Group of the European People's Party and European Democrats (centre-right/right wing)

PES: Group of the Party of European Socialists (centre-left)

ELDR: Group of the European Liberal, Democratic and Reformist Party

GREENS/EFA: Group of the Greens/European Free Alliance (includes regionalists/nationalists)

EUL/NGL: Confederal Group of the European United Left/Nordic Green Left (left and communist parties)

UEN: Group of the Union for a Europe of Nations (anti-EU, mostly from the right)

EDD: Europe of Democracies and Diversities Group

TDI: Technical Group of Independent Members – Mixed Group

NI: Not members of any group

Source: European Parliament.

(organised as the European People's Party). The three medium-sized groups made up of liberals, greens and parties to the left of social democracy will find it difficult to maintain their proportionate strength. Nice also provided for the establishment and possible funding of 'Political Parties at European Level'. Anti-integrationists worry that this may be used to line the pockets of pro-EU parties. Such parties 'contribute to forming a European awareness', which is hardly a neutral form of words, although they also play a role in 'expressing the political will of the citizens of the Union', which appears to leave the door open to just about any tendency. The Treaty merely states that the Council, by QMV, 'shall lay down the regulations governing political parties at European level and in particular the rules regarding their funding'. As governments tend to be from either the PES or PPE tradition this could clearly be manipulated to benefit these two dominant tendencies. The presence of liberals, greens, Communists and other small parties in coalitions in many member states may help prevent this, but such a vague mandate remains blatantly undemocratic.

The European Parliament's original function was consultative. Since 1970, however, it has exercised real power over the budget. In addition, the Treaties of Maastricht and Amsterdam extended a power of co-decision introduced in 1987 with the Single European Act. Co-decision has made the Parliament an important part of the European Union's legislative process. The claim, heard from both opponents and supporters of integrationism, that the European Parliament is toothless, or a talking shop, is out of date.

How it chooses to use its power is another matter. Despite attempts to woo the citizens of the member states with much self-promotion, criticism of the secrecy and elitism of the other institutions, and innovations such as the appointment of an Ombudsman to look after their interests, the EP is unloved and largely ignored. The Parliament, though it includes opponents of the EU and 'Eurosceptics', has a built-in majority of sometimes quite extreme integrationist tendencies, hardly reflecting the reality of political opinion across the member states. Its major point of embarrassment is the very low turn-out at elections: in 1999 fewer than 50 per cent of eligible voters bothered to turn up. Clearly, the keener one is on the EU, the greater the chance of participation, and this distorts the make-up of the Parliament.

Part of the reason for this may be that, as the assembly's power has grown, so has the interest and influence of corporate lobbying.

Scandinavians, in particular, are shocked by the openness with which members will declare that they have had, for example 'representations from industry' over a particular proposal. The most powerful committees, those which deal with the majority of co-decision proposals – principally Environment and Transport – are often held before packed public galleries. Members' hapless assistants are advised to turn up early if they want a seat, though once the item touching the interests of car manufacturers, the chemical industry or Big Oil is dealt with there will invariably be a stampede for the door reminiscent of a zoo when the man with the bucket appears. Plenary assemblies, which occur roughly once a month at Strasbourg and less frequently, and in a shorter form, at Brussels, are also accompanied by huge lobbying efforts. As for the members, some would get marks for honesty if, like footballers, they wore the names of their corporate sponsors on their shirts.

THE EUROPEAN COURT OF JUSTICE

The Court of Justice (ECJ) is made up of one representative from each member state, appointed by 'common accord of the governments of the Member States' for six-year terms. The Justices choose a President from amongst their number. He or she serves a three-year term but may be re-elected. The ECJ's official function is to ensure that European Union law is applied, and applied uniformly, in each of the member states, so that it reinforces the Commission's work of monitoring and policing the application of directives and regulations, as well as the treaties themselves. The Court is assisted by Advocates-General, which it appoints. In addition, the European Court of First Instance exists to hear more routine cases and reduce the ECJ's considerable workload, speeding up the notoriously long process from complaint to judgement.

Comparable in some ways to the US Supreme Court, its much more recent origins and the controversial, supra-national nature of the European Union mean that the ECJ lacks that body's prestige. Many important areas of law, of course – particularly criminal law – remain under the control of the member states, limiting the visibility of the Court to ordinary citizens. To most people, the Court, if they have heard of it at all, appears remote and bureaucratic, unconnected to their everyday lives. The tendency to confuse it with the Council of Europe's European Court of Human Rights (ECHR) is so widespread that many Euro-MPs keep a stack of ECHR application forms to hand to send to constituents who enquire about it.

This indifference is increasingly misconceived. Unlike the ECHR, the ECJ has real power. New laws are often open to a range of interpretations, as is the Treaty, and this gives the last word to the Court. It can even declare a law invalid if it views it as conflicting with the Union's obligations under the Treaty; mirroring this, it can also bring proceedings against the Commission or Council if it fails to act in fulfilment of such obligations.

This power of interpretation has enabled the ECJ to function rather in the way of the World Trade Organisation, with far more direct power and on the basis of much the same principles. A member state can, according to the Treaties, exclude imports on the grounds that they contradict policies and laws designed to protect the consumer or the environment, but it is incumbent on the member state, if challenged by a would-be importer, to prove that it is not hiding the foul fiend of protectionism behind the angel of responsible government.

The European Court of Justice can, not surprisingly, be criticised on much the same grounds as can the courts of most member states. Minorities are unrepresented and women few and far between. No figures are kept on the social backgrounds of the justices, but they naturally tend to be men who have reached the peak of a particular profession and can hardly be said to be representative. Yet they have the power to overturn laws which have been made or upheld by democratically elected national governments.

OTHER EUROPEAN UNION INSTITUTIONS

As well as the Commission, Council, Parliament and Court of Justice the EU's institutional structure comprises a number of lesser-known bodies. Some come under the public eye less often because their duties are internal, technical or more limited in application. The European Court of Auditors, as its name suggests, exists to ensure financial probity amongst the institutions. Its Annual Report does tend to give it a brief yearly notoriety, largely because it invariably takes the form of a catalogue of waste, excess and downright fraud, making it the favourite reading of many an anti-EU journalist. Its members are appointed by the Council by unanimous vote, and their number is the same as that of the member states.

The Economic and Social Committee (ESC, or ECOSOC) represents what in the excruciating euro-jargon are termed the 'social partners', otherwise known as employers and trade unions. Its members are appointed by the Council and divide into the Employers' Group or Group I, the Workers' Group (Group II) and the splendidly titled Various Interests Group, which includes representatives of agriculture, small and medium-sized enterprises (SMEs), the professions and 'skilled trades' and a number of people from interest groups representing, *inter alia*, consumers, environmentalists, family interests and so on. ECOSOC has no power, only the right to be consulted, and its official 'opinions' are generally ignored by everyone who isn't actually a member of it. The Nice Treaty attempted to increase ECOSOC's democratic credibility by broadening representation, now defined as 'representatives of the various economic and social components of organised civil society' with 'consumers' added to the rather quaint list of groups to be included: 'producers, farmers, carriers, workers, dealers, craftsmen, professional occupations ... and the general public'. Its membership before Nice was the mystical-sounding 222, but the new Treaty prepared for enlargement by defining a formula for the Committee's growth to a maximum of 350.

ECOSOC has been around as long as the Community itself. Not so the Union's other talking shop, the Committee of the Regions (CoR). Its members are appointed by the Council on proposals from each member state. In common with ECOSOC, the CoR has absolutely no power, merely the right to be consulted. Its members are taken from local authorities and, where they exist, regional governments. As with ECOSOC, Nice provided a formula for increasing the CoR's size as new member states are admitted, to a maximum of 350.

4 How the European Union Makes Law

The powers and responsibilities of the European Union (its 'competence') are defined in the Treaty of Rome and subsequent amendments. From its inception, the Community had responsibility for the common policies, most importantly covering agriculture, fisheries and international trade. Added to these original responsibilities have been such matters as transport, environmental protection, consumer protection and public health, research and development, the promotion of economic and social cohesion, and co-operation with developing countries.

This growth in power and influence has come about through both formal and informal means. In other words, in some cases competences which were in the original Treaty of Rome were scarcely exercised, usually because of political problems stemming from the national interests of the member states. In some cases, the Union has simply found itself in a situation in which it can exercise in practice powers that it has always enjoyed in theory. In addition, with each formal step in integration new competences have been added.

DIFFERENT SORTS OF LAW

European Union laws take various forms. The most important is probably the Directive, which sets out a policy objective but requires national legislation to implement, or 'transpose'. This gives a certain amount of leeway to the member states and allows for differing conditions, as well, inadvertently perhaps, for different degrees of enthusiasm. The usual two-year time limit is often breached by countries who opposed or were lukewarm about a particular Directive, or when laws are written which do not truly embody a Directive's requirements. In such cases the ECJ has the final word, but court cases also take time, of course, and may allow a member state to delay fulfilling its responsibilities.

Regulations apply immediately throughout the territory of the Union, without requirement for national implementing legislation.

Decisions are also binding, but unlike Regulations and Directives they apply only to the body or bodies to whom they are addressed, which may be a member state, or a legal person (usually a corporation) or natural person (you and me). The EU institutions may have a certain amount of leeway in deciding which sort of law is appropriate in which case, but in reality this is usually dictated by the Treaties.

In addition to these three legislative instruments, the Union or its institutions have a number of non-binding measures at their disposal. A Recommendation is issued by the Commission or by the Council but does not bind member states: again, its name speaks for itself. An Opinion also requires little explanation. Finally, the Commission may issue official Communications stating its views, the Council may make Declarations, and the Parliament issues a constant stream of resolutions dealing with issues over which it has no real power, but where it hopes to exercise influence. Every session of the Parliament passes resolutions on human rights, for example, or crises which are beyond its reach. It has entire committees which deal with no legislative proposals at all, except through the consultation procedure, simply because it does not have competence in those areas.

Each of the institutions described in the previous chapter has a role to play in the creation and implementation of European Union law. Just what that role is is usually determined by the type of law being made, the policy area being crucial. For every proposed law there must be a treaty base. In other words, the Commission, which is the source of new legislative proposals, must be able to cite an Article in the Treaty which gives the EU authority to make laws in that specific policy area. This 'treaty base' can be challenged before the Court of Justice, which has the final say as to whether or not it is legitimate.

The choice of treaty base is crucial, because on it will depend which of the various legislative procedures is used, and therefore the extent of influence of the European Parliament and whether the Council, in approving, rejecting or amending the proposal, must do so by unanimity or by a majority weighted to reflect the population size of each member state, known as Qualified Majority Voting or QMV.

Under QMV, each member state has a certain number of votes, depending on its population size. Smaller states have proportionally more votes. To prepare for enlargement, the Treaty of Nice had to come up with a formula to satisfy everyone: the bigger states wanted a closer link between size and number of votes, whilst the smaller states would accept this only if other safeguards were put in place. In the end, a system was devised which was so complicated that it was still being argued over months later. The provisional distribution of votes was blatantly unfair to some countries, which received fewer votes than others of the same size. References to absolute numbers of votes and percentages did not add up, and the Council would need to appoint an Official Mathematician to advise it as to who had won votes.

The Treaty gives a weighting of votes for each member state and applicant, but these constitute no more than a negotiating position and may be adjusted as applicants prepare for membership. It then gives three separate means of deciding a winning vote, depending on whether it is a proposal from the Commission ('at least 258 votes ... cast by a majority of members'), in other cases ('at least 258 votes ... cast by at least two-thirds'); and finally, the *pièce de résistance:* 'When a decision is to be adopted by the Council by a qualified majority, a member of the Council may request verification that the Member States constituting the qualified majority represent at least 62 per cent of the total population of the Union.' As if this weren't enough, an annexed 'Declaration' states that as more applicants are admitted, the percentage demanded in this test will rise 'until it reaches a maximum of 73.4 per cent'.

QMV is a tremendously politically loaded issue. It is now argued that, because the Union will soon comprise over 20 states, the requirement for unanimity would make it impossible to make any further 'progress'. Whether true or not, this is hardly an argument in the system's favour. QMV means that laws which are opposed by a sovereign state's government and may be abhorrent to its people can be imposed upon them. There may be defences of this, but practicality simply will not do. Dictatorship has always been quicker and more practical than that tiresome business of asking the people what they want.

Majority voting has been extended to new areas at every amendment of the Treaty since the Single European Act. Although the integrationists pronounced themselves 'disappointed' by it, Nice continued this process. After four successive extensions of QMV, only the most politically sensitive issues – defence operations, most tax matters, cultural policy amongst them – are left requiring unanimity.

THE LEGISLATIVE PROCEDURES

There are now four main legislative procedures: consultation, co-operation, co-decision and assent. In addition, there is a special procedure for the annual budget.

Proposals generally begin life on the desk (or screen) of someone at the Commission, though they are often issued at the request of the Council, or because the Treaty obliges it. Before sending a proposal to the Council, and, where required, the Parliament, the Commission generally conducts a wide exercise of consultation. It does this, in many cases, by issuing a Green Paper, followed by a White Paper. These present the Commission's opinion on a given subject and invite interested parties to make their opinions known. Green Papers propose the first ideas for discussion in a specific field where a Community action might be envisaged, often presenting a range of alternative approaches. White Papers set out more detailed suggestions. Having weighed up the various responses, the Commission then makes a formal proposal for what it sees as an appropriate measure.

The most complicated legislative procedure, and the one which gives the greatest influence to the European Parliament, is known as 'co-decision'. Under co-decision, a proposal for a Directive (for example) is sent by the Commission to the Council and Parliament. The Parliament may propose amendments which are then sent to the Council. If the Council accepts the amendments, they are incorporated into the directive. If it rejects any of them, however (and instant agreement is the exception), or introduces any amendments of its own, then the proposal (with any accepted amendments incorporated) returns to the Parliament for a second reading. The document returned to the Parliament reflects a consensus within the Council and is known as the Common Position. The Parliament may then represent its original amendments, reject or change Council's amendments, or present entirely new amendments. It may, however, present new amendments only if circumstances have changed since the first reading (for example, in a Directive dealing with pollution, new scientific discoveries may have been made justifying the placing or removing of restrictions on a particular product or process).

The Council will next consider the results of Parliament's second reading. If it does not accept any of the newly proposed amendments (provided they are legitimate), a Conciliation Committee – made up of equal numbers of members of Parliament and the Council, with the Commission present as an observer, and sometimes to propose compromises – is appointed. Its job is to draw up a joint text that the Council and Parliament may adopt, with the matter then going to a full meeting of each body for final approval. If no agreement can be found, Parliament can reject the proposal outright. If it does so, however, the whole process must begin again with a new proposal from the Commission. For this reason, conciliations, which are becoming increasingly common, can last deep into the night

The co-operation procedure is similar to co-decision in that it enables the Parliament to amend a Commission proposal. This again requires two readings by Parliament. As there is no provision for conciliation, however, and as it gives the last word to the Council, co-operation gives the EP much less power and influence than does co-decision.

Both co-decision and co-operation encourage the formation of alliances across and between the institutions. Under co-decision, governments can work closely with MEPs from their own parties or who happen to share their views on a certain issue. With co-operation, if the Commission and Parliament agree on amendments, the text can be adopted by a Qualified Majority at Council. This means that, if the two institutions and an effective voting majority of member states agree, an amended proposal becomes law. If, however, the Commission rejects the Parliament's amendments, the Council must adopt the proposal unanimously, so that an alliance of one recalcitrant member state (even tiny Luxembourg will do) and the EP can block a proposed law.

The consultation procedure consists of simply requesting Parliament's opinion before the Council adopts a Commission proposal for legislation. It gives the Parliament no formal power whatsoever, but can sometimes (depending on the balance of power and opinion within the other institutions, especially the Council) give it a certain influence.

Finally, the assent procedure's name is self-explanatory. The assent of the Parliament is required, for example, when new member states are admitted or association agreements signed with third countries. As it gives no power to amend, assent is something of a blunt instrument, rather like the power to sack the Commission. The Parliament has attempted to use it to put pressure on certain countries – notably Israel and Turkey – to improve human rights, but all it can do is threaten to withhold consent, or delay giving consent in order to cause inconvenience.

THE BUDGET

The Budget is dealt with under a special procedure which, even before the Parliament first became a directly-elected body in 1979, gave it considerable power. Certainly, before the introduction of the co-operation procedure in the Single European Act of 1987, it was in relation to the annual European Community budget that the EP became most like a normal legislative body.

Before explaining this procedure, it may be worth asking some questions about the end result. Where does the money come from, and how is it spent?

Despite the European Union's justified reputation as a costly and extravagant collection of institutions and practices, its ability to raise its own funds is extremely limited, and its expenditure amounts to only 2.8 per cent of overall GDP. There are four sources of tax revenue which go directly to Brussels: customs duties on imports; levies on agricultural imports, including a special levy on sugar; a contribution based on VAT revenue in all the member states, which represents nearly 42 per cent of 'own resources' – the term used for money which goes by right to the EU (which, as we shall see, is in fact less than half of the Union's income); and a 'fourth resource', based on the gross national product (GNP) of each member state, which represents 40 per cent of funds and ensures a balanced budget.

Roughly speaking, then, member states contribute to the budget in line with their ability to pay, assessed on the basis of various criteria, such as the level of economic development, population and per capita GNP. However, direct payments to support agriculture distort this, by favouring countries where proportionally more people work on the land. In the early 1980s member states agreed that the United Kingdom, which has a very low proportion of its workforce engaged in farming, would get an annual rebate as it was accepted that its net contribution to the EU budget was disproportionate.

Agricultural differences are not the only problem, however. The levy on VAT also fails to produce a fair reflection of member states' wealth. VAT rates vary, so that the proportion of Gross National Product (GNP) collected also varies. This effect is exacerbated by the fact that while some states choose to use VAT exemptions to alleviate poverty or encourage certain kinds of spending (UK exclusions include food, children's clothing and books) others, such as Denmark, impose a flat rate, using other mechanisms to redistribute wealth. The VAT levy is by far the most important source of direct income, bringing in 41 per cent of total revenue in 1998.

Because own resources do not meet the whole of the EU's budgetary needs, since 1988 they have been supplemented by a direct levy based on member states' GNP. In order to offset the distorting effects of differential VAT rates, this levy varies according to the amount of the shortfall once other own resources have been calculated. In 1998 it amounted to 43 per cent of the total EU budget.

Also since 1988, 'own resources' may not exceed a certain percentage of the total of all member states' GNP. This began at 1.15 per cent but has twice been raised, so that it now stands at 1.27 per cent. Because the shortfall is made up by a levy which directly relates to each nation's wealth, the cap on own resources is 'progressive', not in the broad political sense but by the narrower definition applied when discussing taxation: it makes the final total contribution made by each member state more proportionate to its total financial resources.

Spending these resources is, not surprisingly, governed by a complex bureaucratic procedure.

Firstly, on the basis of what is required by the various treaties and legislation derived from them, spending is divided into 'compulsory expenditure' and 'non-compulsory expenditure'. Under the first comes most Common Agricultural Policy (CAP) spending: price support expenditure under the Guarantee section of the European Agricultural Guarantee and Guidance Fund (EAGGF) and some structural spending. In addition, similar expenditure under the Common Fisheries Policy (CFP) is compulsory in this sense, as are direct monetary refunds to the member states and some development aid. Following recent reforms, non-compulsory spending now accounts for a majority of the budget – around 55 per cent in 2000. Unless some unexpected change occurs, this trend will continue, and, as foreseen in *Agenda 2000*, the Commission's blueprint for the development of the Union, compulsory expenditure should continue to take up a diminishing proportion of resources.

THE BUDGETARY PROCEDURE

Before 1970, the Council alone decided how much would be spent on what. Since the Budgetary Treaty of 1970, amended and enhanced by a further treaty in 1975, the European Parliament has, together with the Council, formed what is known as the budgetary authority. Whereas before 1970 it had the right only to be consulted, it now has a statutory and quite powerful role in the procedure. The first Budgetary Treaty gave it the final say over non-compulsory expenditure, while the 1975 Treaty enabled it to throw out the entire budget. In practice, Parliament's power, though extensive, is limited by both informal pressure – failure to agree a budget could result in chaos – and formal restrictions. In particular, the Commission is able each year to determine a maximum which serves as a guideline to the extent to which expenditure may be increased in relation to the previous annual budget. This is done on the basis of three parameters: the growth of the total GNP of the member states; the average growth (or reduction) in member states' own national annual budgets; and the overall EU inflation rate. This guideline is not binding, however. The budgetary authority may exceed it, but only if Parliament and Council together agree to do so.

Although agriculture takes a declining share of the total budget, it remains by far the biggest item. In 1998, it took almost half of the Union's spending (49 per cent), as opposed to just over a third (34.2 per cent) for the Structural Funds. Other internal policies took a mere 5.6 per cent, external spending 5.4 per cent and administration 3.4 per cent. Expenditure is also governed by multi-annual guidelines agreed between the member states and the budgetary authority.

As with almost all important EU business, the budget, drawn up annually, begins life as a Commission proposal. This proposal, known as the 'preliminary draft budget' (PDB) is drawn up in keeping with guidelines laid down by the budgetary authority – the Council and Parliament. The PDB for the following year is first sent to the Council, where it must arrive at the latest by 1 September – which means that at least one group of Commission employees is forced to defy the stereotype and spend the summer in a Brussels otherwise given over to tourists.

The Council, acting by qualified majority, considers the Commission's proposal and adopts a modified version of it, known as the 'draft budget'. It has until 5 October to forward this to the Parliament. Parliament then has 45 days to adopt the budget or demand amendments. If, in that time, it fails to state a position, the budget is deemed to have been adopted. In practice, however, the Parliament sends the budget back within the stated period and requests amendments.

If the Parliament proposes changes to compulsory expenditure, it must do so by a majority of votes cast; if, however, the changes affect non-compulsory expenditure, they must be adopted under the system which requires the approval of an absolute majority of all members, not just those who happen to have taken time off from busy lives to attend Strasbourg.

Once the Council has received the Parliament's proposals, it has 15 days in which to conduct what is called its 'second reading'. If it accepts all of the Parliament's proposed changes, the budget is adopted. If it does not, what happens next depends on the nature of the amendments. The crucial question is this: would a Parliament proposal require an increase in overall EU expenditure? If the answer is no, then the Council must reject or modify it by QMV, and if this does not happen it becomes part of the budget. If the answer is yes, then it must adopt it by QMV, and if a qualified majority cannot be found to accept it, then it falls. If the Council is willing to accept an amendment only in modified form, then it must send its (now final) proposal back to the Parliament.

It is now Parliament's turn to move swiftly. Within 15 days, it must conduct its own second reading, and if it misses this tight deadline, the Council's proposed compromise amendments are integrated into the budget and the budget adopted. Here, for once, the Parliament really does have the last word, however, though conditions governing the exercise of this power are stringent. Now, in order to amend or reject the Council's final proposal, it must find not only an absolute majority of all members, but also three-fifths of those who actually turn up to vote.

This vote completes the budgetary process, and the budget becomes law after it is taken – unless (didn't you somehow know there would be an 'unless'?) Parliament, on the basis of the same double majority, votes to reject the whole thing. In this event, the entire show must restart on the basis of a new proposal from the Commission. If no agreement is reached before 1 January, the Union must finance its activities through a system known as 'provisional twelfths'. An idea borrowed from the United States' federal government, this means that an appropriation is made each month which is equivalent to one-twelfth of the previous year's budget.

Obviously, this can cause difficulties. Even a low rate of inflation requires some adjustment of the budget, but the provisional twelfths take no account of this. Nor does the system make allowance for the fact that spending is not evenly distributed throughout the year. The potential problems arising from this mean that pressure builds on the Parliament to accept something less than the fulfilment of its every dream. The pro-EU press invariably presents the resulting agreement as a sign of Parliament's 'growing maturity'. Less kind voices complain that it is yet another example of the assembly's tendency to be all gong and no dinner.

Monitoring Expenditure

It is one thing to fix a budget and another to make sure that it is spent honestly and as intended. Again, the European Parliament has a relatively major role to play in this, through its Committee on Budgetary Control. This conducts on its behalf an annual assessment of the management of the budget before giving, on the basis of the Annual Report of the Court of Auditors, its approval, formally termed a 'discharge'. As with the budget procedure itself, during the debate over the discharge the Parliament generally makes a tremendous fuss, but everything comes out all right in the end.

5 Enlargement

Since its foundation in 1957 by the original Six, the European Community (later the Union) has grown through a succession of enlargements to its present tally of 15 members. The admission of the United Kingdom, Ireland and Denmark in 1973 was followed in 1981 by the accession of Greece, and in 1986 by that of Spain and Portugal. In 1995 these countries were joined by Austria, Finland and Sweden.

The EU's official policy is 'to welcome any European state which wishes to join'. Beyond that, the Union's institutions take a decidedly lofty view of the process of enlargement, describing it as having 'an unprecedented political, historical and moral dimension'. The spread of the Union is seen as akin to an evangelical episode which will '(bring) our continent together. We are moving from division to unity, from a propensity for conflict to stability, and from economic inequality to better life-chances in the different parts of Europe.' Before this can happen, however, a number of problems, acknowledged (though with rather different emphases and conclusions) on all sides, must be overcome.

Integrationists worry that larger will inevitably mean shallower, that a Union of 20 or more member states will end up as nothing more than a free-trade area marred by endless wrangling, with all possibility of 'progress' stalled by the difficulty of finding agreement on anything but the most general level. Greens and those on the left, on the other hand, are concerned by what seems to be a tendency to put social and environmental questions on the back seat. The Commission itself admits that, with some exceptions, 'adoption of the *acquis* continues to be slow in the social policy and employment sector', while although 'the transposition of environment *acquis* has started to progress faster in a number of countries', much 'remains to be done ... for both *acquis* alignment and implementation capacity' in this field.[1]

Institutional matters also present difficulties. The question of the balance of power between states, of just how much acknowledgement should be given to national independence and sovereignty and how much to the realities of population size – in other words, how much majority voting should there be and what should constitute

a 'majority' – is potentially explosive. Larger countries resent the disproportionate voting strengths given to smaller member states, while
the latter fear domination by the giants. The gap between the richest
members and the poorest will widen with the admission of a large
number of countries which are poorer than any already in. Then, if
all the political and economic problems are successfully addressed,
the horrendous task remains of devising an institutional structure
which will allow this mega-Union to function, and one which gives
at least the appearance of being democratic. Anyone who has seen
the European Parliament working in eleven languages will be able
to imagine the chaos which could so easily descend were a further
nine or so to be added. Even if some constitutional genius were able
to devise a working system, it would inevitably be extremely
expensive, a major consideration for a body which is already
conscious of its waning popularity.

The fall of Communism created, almost overnight, a large number
of potential EU members. As we have seen, though the Treaty offers
some leeway with regard to details, it makes it quite clear that the
'free market' – the now politically correct term for capitalism – is the
fundamental and unchangeable system by which EU member states
must conduct their affairs. European Union membership, which
continues to enjoy widespread (if declining in some countries)
support throughout the applicant states, is regarded as a way out of
an impasse which has seen a stagnant and repressive state socialism
replaced by a capitalist system marked by criminality and the
absence of the sort of checks and balances which have evolved in
much of the west. Almost everywhere, incompetence, corruption
and nepotism reign supreme.

Also to be considered, of course, are what the implications of
enlargement might be for the existing Union. When EU Commissioner Verheugen suggested that referenda on the desirability or
otherwise of enlargement might not be inappropriate, he was repri-
manded, ridiculed and reviled from almost all sides.[2] Why this
should be so is unclear, given the Union's much-trumpeted
commitment to democracy and involvement. For the consequences
of enlargement, if they are huge for the applicant countries, are
hardly negligible for the current member states.

What the reality of westward migration might turn out to be in an
enlarged Union – to take just one area of widespread concern – is
difficult to say. The balance of probabilities is that it would make
little difference to numbers, merely legitimising the position of the

Table 5.1 Candidate Countries, Main Statistical Indicators, 1999

	Area	Population	GDP in P.P.S. Purchasing Power Standards><1		
	1000 km²	Million inhabitants	Billion € P.P.S.	€/inhab. P.P.S.	€/inhab. % EU average
Bulgaria	111	8,3	38,5	4700	22
Cyprus	9	0,7	12,0	17100	81
Czech Rep.	79	10,3	128,7	12500	59
Estonia	45	1,4	10,8	7800	36
Hungary	93	10,1	108,1	10700	51
Latvia	65	2,4	13,9	5800	27
Lithuania	65	3,7	22,9	6200	29
Malta	0,3	0,4	n.a.	n.a.	n.a.
Poland	313	38,7	301,9	7800	37
Romania	238	22,5	128,2	5700	27
Slovakia	49	5,4	55,6	10300	49
Slovenia	20	2,0	30,0	15000	71
Turkey	775	64,3	379,4	5900	28

	Inflation rate Annual Average	Unemployment rate International Labour Organisation Definition % active population	exp⇒EU in % total exports	imp⇐EU in per cent total imports
Bulgaria	2,6	17,0	52,6	48,6
Cyprus	1,3	3,6	50,7	57,3
Czech Rep.	2,0	8,7	69,2	64,0
Estonia	4,6	11,7	72,7	65,0
Hungary	10,0	7,0	76,2	64,4
Latvia	2,4	14,5	62,5	54, 5
Lithuania	0,8	14,1	50,1	49,7
Malta	2,1	5,3	48,7	65,4
Poland	7,2	15,3	70,5	64,9
Rumania	45,8	6,8	65,5	60,4
Slovakia	10,6	16,2	59,4	51,7
Slovenia	6,1	7,6	66,0	68,6
Turkey	64,9	7,6	52,6	53,9

Note: 1998 figures based on 1€ = $1,066 US; except trade figures which are from a different original source and based on a slightly earlier 1998 rate 1€ = $1,122.

Source: Eurostat figures posted at the website of the Austrian research organisation SAIS at http://www.eue.org/.

large numbers of CEE citizens currently living in EU member states illegally.

Reality is one thing, however, and the manipulations of the extreme right quite another. We have already seen, with the rise of Haider in Austria, the way in which the creation of an unrestricted eastern border could be used by the far right to attract support. The right has discovered that, by playing on fears of an influx of cheap labour and organised crime, it has been able to attract votes.

The Commission's view that a further benefit to existing member states will come from the creation of 'an enlarged Single Market with the introduction of rapidly growing economies' is simple wishful thinking. By its own estimate, accession of even those applicant countries most likely to be admitted in the first wave will increase the EU's population by over 25 per cent – to 500 million – 'while total GDP will grow by no more than 5 per cent'. True, the existing member states 'run considerable surpluses on their export trade with the candidate countries', but the candidates will surely expect a successful accession to reduce these surpluses rather than increase them.[3]

The phrase 'rapidly growing economies' is, to put it kindly, misleading. The 1999 average real growth rate for the Central and East European candidates was 2.2 per cent – healthy enough in most circumstances, but hardly breathtaking in its rapidity. Moreover, this average, as is always the case, disguised huge differences. The three Baltic states each continued their miserable post-Soviet economic performance, with rates varying from +0.1 per cent to –4.1 per cent. Turkey's 5 per cent decline could be at least partly blamed on a major earthquake, but Romania also declined heavily while the Czech Republic's –0.1 per cent was an improvement on previous years. Only Slovenia (4.9 per cent), Hungary (4.5 per cent), and Poland (4.2 per cent) of the CEE candidates, plus Malta at 4.2 per cent, could be described as experiencing rapid growth.[4]

As well as possible economic difficulties and the bogey of 'uncontrollable immigration', the Commission admits to considerable potential problems and lists as 'fears about possible negative impact of enlargement' the following: 'unfair competition, particularly for jobs, imported crime, environmental dumping … financial burdens … (and) that the EU might be incapable after an enlargement on such a scale of properly achieving its objectives'. Typically, its answer to such fears is not an adjustment of policy, but simply to improve its 'communication strategy'.[5]

As for the applicant countries, the benefits of membership are, at the very least, accompanied by a number of risks which are rarely acknowledged in the official propaganda. The conditions under which a membership application will be successful are known as the Copenhagen Criteria. Each country must demonstrate that it is a democracy living under the rule of law, showing respect for human rights and the protection of minorities; that it has a functioning market economy, an ability to cope with competitive pressures within the Single Market and accept the obligations of membership, including the rules known as the *acquis communautaire*, a body of law with some 20,000 pieces of legislation.

Each of these conditions raises questions of considerable concern, though the details vary greatly from one applicant country to another. Democracy and the rule of law, as defined within the political traditions of the west, are now more-or-less established, with multiparty elections, a nominally free press, and a judiciary with some claims to independence from other branches of the state. According to the Commission: 'all currently negotiating candidate countries met (in 1999) the political criteria, even if some still had progress to make in the protection of human rights and minorities'. This was an optimistic view, however, and did not include Turkey, with whom negotiations had not begun.

Market economies function, though not always quite to the degree demanded by the Treaty or in the way their supporters claim. The Commission itself draws attention to a continuing 'serious problem' of corruption. Other problems cited include 'trafficking in women and children' and legally sanctioned gender discrimination.[6]

PAYING FOR ENLARGEMENT

The EU has been criticised for the limited degree to which it has offered financial and other forms of support to enable the applicant countries to meet the exacting criteria. In March 1999, the member states responded to this criticism by allocating a total of €3 billion for the period 2000–06. Of this, €1.5b is to be distributed through the PHARE programme , 1b through a structural support programme modelled on the existing Structural Funds (ISPA), and 500m to provide agricultural support.

These billions were not, however, added to the EU budget but merely reallocated from other lines. This pleased the rich, powerful member states who were already heavy net contributors and went some way to placating anti-EU opinion within those countries. It was not so welcome to less wealthy members such as Greece and Portugal, however, who now found themselves having to compete for effectively decreased resources with countries with large agricultural sectors and whose GDP was lower – in some cases far lower – than their own.

The main sources of finance for the candidate countries are known as the 'pre-accession instruments'. They perform the same functions as will the Structural Funds (described in Chapters 11 and 15) if and when these countries become members. ISPA (Instrument for Structural Policies for Pre-Accession Aid) pays for transport and environmental projects. PHARE (Poland–Hungary Assistance in Restructuring their Economies) is designed to support the adoption and application of the *acquis* and to reinforce administrative and judicial capacity. Despite its name, it is now open to all of the candidate countries. SAPARD (Special Action for Pre-Accession measures for Agriculture and Rural Development) provides support for improving the 'efficiency' of farms, promoting high value-added products and vocational training.

Candidate countries can also participate to varying degrees in EC programmes and agencies, including the Socrates educational exchange programme, LIFE (which provides support for nature conservation), and the Fifth Framework Programme for Research and Technological Development. Negotiations regarding the details of participation in these and other programmes are ongoing. The Union is keen to encourage participation in its various 'Agencies', such as the European Environment Agency, negotiations regarding which were completed towards the end of 2000.

By 1999, 13 countries were fully involved in the enlargement process: Bulgaria, Cyprus, Czech Republic, Estonia, Hungary, Latvia, Lithuania, Malta, Poland, Romania, Slovak Republic, Slovenia and Turkey. Each had signed an 'Accession Partnership' agreement and entered what was known as 'the pre-accession strategy', though the last of these, with Cyprus and Malta, were not finalised until March, 2000.

SCREENING

The Commission produces an annual report dealing with each country and based on what is called 'screening'. Screening takes us past generalities about the 'market economy' and 'democracy' and into the realm of detail. In the screening process, the EU *acquis* is used as the yardstick against which an applicant's 'progress' is measured. For this purpose, the *acquis* is divided into 31 'chapters' – areas of law dealing with different aspects of policy, such as the CAP, environmental protection, foreign policy (the CFSP) and so on. The idea is that a new member will not be admitted until it has complied with this *acquis*, adapting its laws and practices to those approved by the Treaty of Rome. Though in some cases 'transitional measures' may be allowed – exceptional areas in which a particular Directive or Regulation need not be applied – these must be limited in duration and accompanied by reasoned explanations. Nevertheless, by late 2000 the Commission had received over 500 requests for such arrangements, the vast majority of them relating to agriculture.

The EU has also been criticised for expecting this adaptation to be a simple one-way process. There is no question of the Union adapting itself in any way to these new members, other than by institutional changes which are unavoidable if the process is not to bring chaos or paralysis. The message is clear. Everything that happens in the EU is better than everything that happens outside it. If countries want to join, the Union will certainly change, but only to ensure its own survival, not to take advantage of any strengths the applicants may have. Nothing can possibly be learnt.

A further criticism concerns the lack, or exceedingly changeable nature, of any accession timetable. As the Commission itself admits, the 'complex negotiating process, coupled with the difficult preparation for membership, gives rise to uncertainty on the part of the candidate countries about the progress of enlargement'. The failure to set a 'rigid timetable' however, is explained by the fact that: 'the entry criteria have to be fulfilled, and that means a sustained effort of reform that often depends on domestic political and economic circumstances and therefore cannot be worked out in advance.' The threat here is clear. If you elect the wrong kind of government, you're out.[7]

The hope is now that negotiations with the most 'advanced' candidate countries are concluded by the end of 2002. Whether this will turn out to be the case depends on a subtle mixture involving real 'progress' by the applicants, the willingness of the EU and its member states to turn a blind eye in areas where such progress may be more evident on paper than it is in the real world, and the continuing stability of the dangerous, explosive political cocktail which is the aftermath of Soviet hegemony.

TURKEY, CYPRUS AND MALTA

There is always a tendency, when discussing enlargement, to forget that three countries are involved which were never part of that hegemony. Turkey is now officially a candidate state with access to pre-accession instruments. In addition to the economic problems involved in adapting Turkey's traditionally state-directed economy to the Treaty of Rome, concerns centre on the human rights issue. Turkey has by far the worst record of any candidate, is involved in a bloody war of repression in Kurdestan, and is in occupation of part of one of the other candidates! In addition, with a population of 80 million Turkey would rival Germany as the Union's biggest state, which, as it would also be its poorest, might raise some interesting issues. Nevertheless, negotiations continue.

Cyprus has a population of approximately 741,000 inhabitants, made up of the Greek Cypriot community (630,000 inhabitants), the Turkish Cypriot community (89,000 inhabitants) and 22,000 others. The island has been linked to the European Community since 1972 by an association agreement, and applied for membership in 1990. Cyprus easily fulfils the political and economic membership criteria. It is the richest applicant country, with a GDP of over 80 per cent of the EU average, and already does more than half of its trade with the EU. The former occupying power, Britain, continues to maintain a military presence on the island and strong trade links. Cyprus also, of course, enjoys a close relationship with Greece. However, part of its territory is illegally occupied by Turkey and has unilaterally declared itself an independent republic. It is recognised as such only by Turkey. The official accession process has been under way since 1998. In the Commission's stated view, Cyprus has progressed well with adoption of the *acquis*, especially in the Customs Union, but needs to strengthen administration in a number of sectors.

Finally, with 371,000 inhabitants, Malta is the smallest of the States applying for membership. Its attitude to, and even its application for, membership has been an on-off affair, with one of the two major parties, the Labour Party, which alternates in government with the Nationalists (a centre-right party), being historically opposed. Labour won power in 1996, withdrew the membership application lodged in 1990, then lost office after less than two years. Returning to power, the Nationalists 'reactivated' their application. Malta is not poor by pan-European standards and already does most of its trade with the EU. Problems may arise from two of the island's strong traditions: protectionism and neutrality. Malta continues to apply duties to certain EU imports, is unprepared for adaptation to the Common Agricultural Policy, and may have problems with the Common Foreign and Security Policy. The existence of a large and active movement against EU membership could also have its effects.[8]

NICE

The major purpose of the Intergovernmental Conference which culminated with the signing of the Treaty of Nice was supposed to be the facilitation of enlargement. Instead, Nice left a list of unresolved issues, confusing wordings, and bad feelings. Its stipulation of the projected numbers of representatives each country would have in the European Parliament and how many votes each would have at Council under the system of Qualified Majority Voting, for example, made no statistical sense and had to be reopened for debate. To any sufficiently objective observer Nice seemed to have made little or no contribution to solving the various conundrums of enlargement.

6 The Common Foreign and Security Policy

Before Maastricht, the European Community had no real official foreign policy and though foreign ministers of the member states met regularly, they did not do so as the Council but under the aegis of the elaborately-titled Foreign Ministers Meeting in Political Cooperation, with no formal powers. With the end of the Cold War pressures had mounted to abandon the virtual taboo on moves towards a genuinely common foreign policy. Once again, the collapse of the Soviet Union changed everything. When foreign and defence policy were developed within the context of a bipolar world, attitudes to the two 'superpowers' were all-important – and amongst EC member states they differed considerably. Britain was loyally pro-American, France more even-handed, and West Germany had still, to some extent, to do as it was told. Then, in the 1990s, there was suddenly only one superpower.

There were those who dreamed that a united Europe might make it two. Some of the political leaders who flaunt their newly-discovered 'European' credentials as if they were marks of a pacific and well-meaning internationalism are in fact what used to be called Great Power Chauvinists: in place of an all-conquering France, Germany or Britain they favour a strong multinational Greater Europe, with its own army and a relationship with the United States which would recreate the kind of wary respect with which the nineteenth-century Powers eyed each other across the negotiating table. On the other hand, there are elements in the United States which have welcomed the possibility that 'Europe' might at last be able to pay its own defence bills. With the USSR out of the way, large sections of American opinion began to wonder why GIs had to be stationed in Europe at all.

FROM YUGOSLAVIA TO AMSTERDAM

In the 1990s, as change in Central and Eastern Europe gave way to chaos and war, the argument was increasingly heard that if 'Europe' wanted to be taken seriously it must develop an independent capability to respond – politically, diplomatically and ultimately militarily – to crises on its own borders. The break-up of Yugoslavia and the subsequent horrors in Croatia, Bosnia and most recently Kosovo amplified these calls.

The result was Maastricht's creation of the Second Pillar and the replacement of Political Cooperation by a Common Foreign and Security Policy (CFSP). In the urgent context created by the violent disintegration of Yugoslavia, Amsterdam attempted to go further than this, to bring the dream of a united and assertive 'Europe' closer, by extending majority voting in certain areas of foreign policy and, most strikingly perhaps, by providing for the appointment of a High Representative for the CFSP. In 1999, the first appointee to this post, former NATO general secretary Javier Solana Madariaga, the man who had presided over the bombing of Yugoslavia, took office.

In addition, the Amsterdam Treaty provided for the formulation of a common defence force, though not immediately. The Treaty merely empowered the Council to set up such a force should it wish to do so, a decision which must, however, be ratified by every member state. A long-standing but largely moribund defence co-operation organisation, the Western European Union (WEU), became, in effect, the military wing of the EU, with responsibility to draw up and put into practice any decisions with defence implications. Official integration of the WEU into the Union could occur, but again only if ratified by all member states.

By deepening the foreign and defence policy role of the EU, Amsterdam sharpened the Union's military aspects. Its provisions represented a further erosion of the autonomy of the member states, including most disturbingly the four – Austria, Finland, Ireland and Sweden – which had long been neutral. The Treaty made such neutrality difficult if not untenable.

It has been argued that the position of neutral member states is protected by Article J7(1) which states that: 'The policy of the Union in accordance with this Article shall not prejudice the specific character of the security and defence policy of certain Member States and shall respect the obligations of certain Member States, which see their common defence realised in NATO, under the North Atlantic Treaty, and be compatible with the Common Security and Defence Policy established within that framework.'[1] In fact, a careful reading of this Article in the context of the rest of the Treaty demonstrates that it is the latter part of this clause which carries the punch. J7(1) is there to reassure NATO that an emerging EU defence policy will complement, rather than undermine, its own – for which read the USA's – hegemonic role. This is of particular concern to the UK, the second biggest contributor to NATO and the United States' most reliable European ally, or, if you prefer, lapdog.[2]

The fact that one of its open aims was to promote the co-ordination of armaments manufacture is a blatant demonstration that the EU's much-vaunted commitment to peace comes with strings, if not a burning fuse, attached. Recognition of the special, highly political and therefore partly extra-commercial nature of the weapons industry had been under pressure for some time before Amsterdam, both from outright militarists and from those who could not bear to see a sector worth £40 billion a year – fully 2 per cent of EU industrial production, and a workforce of around a million – treated as anything other than just another industry whose competitiveness needed enhancing in the face of growing market pressure from the US and others. As former Industry Commissioner Martin Bangemann said shortly before the Amsterdam Summit: 'The fragmented nature of the European defence industry clearly gives it a competitive disadvantage.'[3]

Amsterdam changed the institutional balance of power, allowing 'the Union' and not the Maastricht formulation's 'Union and its Member States' to 'define and implement a common foreign and security policy'. In addition, the Treaty states that 'the European Council shall define the principles of and general guidelines for the CFSP, *including for matters with defence implications'* (author's italics). The post-Amsterdam CFSP includes the 'progressive' (instead of Maastricht's 'eventual') framing of a common defence policy, 'in accordance' with the WEU.[4]

Moreover, Amsterdam integrates the WEU's responsibility for 'humanitarian and rescue tasks, peacekeeping tasks and tasks of combat forces in crisis management, including peacemaking' – known as the Petersberg tasks after the place where they were originally formulated – into the EU. Whilst the Petersberg tasks may well include worthy and genuinely humanitarian missions, their definition is so wide and vague as to allow almost anything. We live, after all, in the age of 'humanitarian bombing'. If NATO believes that aerial bombardment of civilian populations can be defined as one of the legitimate '(t)asks of combat forces in crisis management, including peacemaking' then the EU and WEU are hardly likely to differ. Moreover, the Treaty's wording, that the common defence policy 'shall include' the Petersberg tasks, implies that there is nothing to prevent the EU from doing whatever else it may choose.[5]

In case anyone was left in any doubt as to what was intended, the 15 heads of state and government, together with the President of the European Commission, responded to the Kosovo crisis and subsequent NATO bombardment by declaring, at a European Council meeting held in June 1999, that: 'the Union must have the capacity for autonomous action, backed up by credible military forces, the means to decide to use them, and a readiness to do so, in order to respond to international crises without prejudice to action by NATO'. Such actions would include, but not be limited to humanitarian and rescue missions, crisis management, and 'peacemaking'.[6]

HOW THE CFSP WORKS

Common foreign and security policy (CFSP) is governed by the provisions of Title V of the Treaty on European Union. The Maastricht Treaty established a three-pillar structure, and Title V constitutes one of the three 'pillars' of the European Union, the others being the European Community and Justice and Home Affairs. Decisions were initially by unanimity, and the Commission, Parliament and ECJ had no competence. Since Amsterdam, however, measures may be adopted by QMV. A state may, however, register a 'constructive abstention', which may include opting out of the action or policy decided upon; or it can use the power of veto, in which case the matter may be referred to the European Council if the member states decide by QMV that they wish to do so. The Commission now has a limited role, mainly in policy implementation.

The European Council is also empowered to define a 'Common Strategy' governing the CFSP approach of the Union in regard to a particular problem. Once a Common Strategy has been defined, it is implemented by the Council of Ministers which is able to take decisions under it using QMV.

The Council is assisted by a High Representative for the CFSP who may also speak for the EU if asked to do so by the Presidency country. The High Representative is in turn assisted by a Planning and Early Warning Unit. The Unit's tasks are to:

- monitor developments in areas relevant to the CFSP;

- provide assessments of the Union's foreign and security policy interests and identify areas on which the CFSP should focus;
- provide timely assessments and early warning of events, potential political crises and situations that might have significant repercussions on the CFSP;
- produce reasoned policy option papers for the Council.[7]

The CFSP opens the way for the EU to develop a common defence, including joint armed forces, should the European Council decide it; and it allows for the integration of the Western European Union (WEU) – the defence organisation which brings together European NATO members – into the European Union.[8]

COMMON (MARKET) VALUES?

The arguments in favour of CFSP, and, by implication, of a European Union military capability, are straightforward. The EU is a strong economic presence in the world, which gives it political interests which must be promoted. Together, the EU and its member states account for more than 50 per cent of both international development aid and humanitarian aid, a third of aid to the Middle East and almost 60 per cent of that which goes to the former Soviet Union. In addition, as we saw in the last chapter, the member states are the major trading partners of their neighbours to the east.

As the CFSP's own website puts it 'The Union must defend the values common to the Fifteen, its fundamental interests, its independence and its security. It must be capable of meeting multiple threats, such as the proliferation of weapons of mass destruction, arms trafficking, contraband nuclear material, fundamentalism and extremism. The emergence of local conflicts, or wars, as in former Yugoslavia, can also destabilise neighbouring States.'[9]

As with so many aspects of the European Union, what tends to irritate opponents of the CFSP or, as they see it, 'militarisation', is the pretence that what is being defended is a common set of values and interests to which all Europeans, and indeed all civilised or decent people, automatically and unquestioningly subscribe. Whether such values can be said to exist at all is a matter of intense philosophical debate and speculation, though never amongst the EU's ruling elites. That they might include a particular version of the market economy is, to say the least, questionable.

Box 6.1

The Five Official Aims of the CFSP – as Defined in the Treaties

- to safeguard the common values, fundamental interests, independence and integrity of the Union in conformity with the principles of the United Nations Charter;
- to strengthen the security of the Union in all ways;
- to preserve peace and strengthen international security, in accordance with the principles of the United Nations Charter, as well as the principles of the Helsinki Final Act and the objectives of the Paris Charter, including those on external borders;
- to promote international co-operation;
- to develop and consolidate democracy and the rule of law, and respect for human rights and fundamental freedoms.

7   Citizenship, Justice and Home Affairs

Apart from monetary union, perhaps the most controversial topic which arose during the debate which preceded the Maastricht Treaty concerned the establishment of a citizenship of the European Union. Following Maastricht, anyone holding nationality of an EU member state became automatically a citizen also of the Union. Why should this be controversial?

Firstly, because it can fairly be cited as substance to the allegation that the EU is on its way to becoming a supra-national state. Only states have citizens. Secondly, because the usual idea of citizenship is that it confers rights and obligations. In this case, however, the rights conferred seem negligible and the obligations, though currently non-existent, something of a blank cheque for future use. The widespread feeling that the EU is remote and beyond the control or even influence of ordinary people is thus accompanied by a fear that things will be demanded of people – taxes? loyalty? military service? – which they have never agreed to make available and which are properly offered only to their country.

'European Union citizenship' is not, in fact, citizenship as usually defined. It does confer certain rights, but they are limited and not those normally associated with nationality. Firstly, and most importantly, it confers the right to move freely within the territory of the Union, which prior to 1990 was conditional on one's being economically active (a worker, or employer, or self-employed person) or a close family member of someone who was one of these. The Single European Act sought to abolish frontier controls, but this proved difficult to implement. In 1990 the right of residence in a member state other than one's own was extended to anyone with sufficient means to support him- or her- self. Two years later this right became an aspect of EU citizenship, finally divorcing it from economic activity. In fact, controls remain at borders going into the UK and Ireland, while the anecdotal evidence for the routine harassment of people of colour by European law enforcement authorities is overwhelming. In addition, during several weeks in 2000, Belgium, having declared an 'amnesty' for *sans papiers* –

unauthorised foreign residents from outside the EU, or 'illegal immigrants' – conducted heavy border controls in order to make sure no one sneaked in to take advantage. This illegal act by the Belgian government was treated rather differently than it would have been had it not been mere human beings who were attempting to cross the border, but something important, such as wine, or bananas. Try keeping *them* out!

Secondly, every national of any member state is entitled, if outside the EU and in a country where his or her nation has no diplomatic representation, to use the embassy and consular services of a member state which does have such facilities. Thirdly, every European Union citizen residing in a member state other than his or her own is entitled to vote in municipal and European Parliament elections under the same conditions as the country's own nationals.

Finally, the right to petition the European Parliament and to apply to the European Ombudsman is something which has been trumpeted as belonging to the rights of the 'European Union citizen'. In fact, most people, if they know of the existence of the office of European Ombudsman at all, or have any idea what the holder of the office can do for them, would probably have taken the right to petition for granted, as they no doubt do in the case of the Parliament.[1] Yet this is clearly not a right of citizenship at all. The right to petition has been enjoyed in many parts of Europe since the middle ages, even by those (such as women and foreigners) who were denied all other forms of political participation. And sure enough, not to be outdone by mediaeval kings or Estates General, the rules governing the Ombudsman make it quite clear than anyone, citizen or not, legally resident in one of the member states, has the right to use his or her services.

THE AMSTERDAM TREATY

The Amsterdam Treaty failed to address the embarrassing lack of substance in this concept of Union citizenship. The only genuinely new right it contained was the stipulation that the European Union 'citizen' would henceforth be able to write to a range of EU institutions in any of the twelve official languages.

Perhaps as important as anything in the words of the Treaty, however, was the fact that for the first time Amsterdam turned member states' attention to the fact that there was widespread dissatisfaction with the EU, as well as a small but vociferous opposition from both left and right which grew from and fed off a suspicion and indifference which in some member states was almost ubiquitous. Trade unionists, the left and far left, Greens and other environmentalists, anarchists, and people from a wide variety of causes and groups, gathered on the streets of Europe's most famously libertarian city. The cosy, closed world of the late twentieth-century power elite was temporarily disrupted. Dutch police officers, previously renowned for their willingness to give you a light (whatever you happened to be smoking), now demonstrated that they were also able to behave in the same unreasonable, bizarre, violent fashion as is normal for their colleagues in many other parts of the world. Reality arrived on the EU's doorstep, and some vague, distant whiff of it even managed to seep past the massed ranks of riot police and under the solid doors of the Amsterdam *Stadhuis*.

The demonstrations, moreover, were the culmination of a long process during which pressure was put on the member state governments and the Commission to offer something more to ordinary people than a flimsy and irrelevant citizenship. This had involved not only earlier street demos and marches but consultations with trade unions and NGOs about what they wanted to see. The result was a series of 'compromises' which established limited new commitments by the EU and its member states.

Before Amsterdam, the EU came under great pressure to make some meaningful commitment to the kind of rights and freedoms to which people are generally presumed to be attached, things which they would feel were more meaningful to their lives than the rather airy concept of 'citizenship' was likely to prove. Much of what was demanded, however, would have meant further extensions of the EU's competence into areas which most member states were not prepared to accept. This meant that, whilst little new was offered, the Treaty stresses the importance of respect for fundamental rights, especially those guaranteed by the Council of Europe's European Convention on Human Rights (ECHR). The *Preamble* of the section of the Amsterdam text known as the European Community Treaty makes reference not only to this Convention but also to the Council of Europe's 1961 European Social Charter and the 1989 Community Charter of the Fundamental Social Rights of Workers, both of which deal mainly with employees' rights.[2]

Whether this had any discernible effects out there in the real world is open to question. According to the Treaty of Amsterdam, the EU has the power to take appropriate action to combat discrimination. Discrimination covers gender, race or ethnic origin, religious and other beliefs, disability, age or sexual orientation. The Commission was required to come up with proposals to give substance to this power, but the result has been many fine words and no real advance. Nothing in the Treaty, nor in what has been suggested since, indicates that the member states are willing to cede control over these areas of policy to any kind of supra-national institution.

The Court of Justice already enjoys some competence to combat discrimination on the grounds of nationality, which has been illegal since the original Treaty of Rome was signed. The Amsterdam Treaty, however, conveys no power to individuals to bring actions relating to other forms of discrimination before the Court if they do not receive redress from the national courts. The sole possible exception – though Amsterdam left the whole area extremely grey indeed – is the formal power given to the ECJ to ensure respect of 'fundamental rights and freedoms' by the EU itself, or its institutions.

There was enough in Amsterdam and in the debate which preceded and followed it, however, to convince decision-makers in the EU and its member states that further steps might be taken to increase the relevance of the Union to ordinary people's lives – or to take further steps towards a superstate with its own supra-national constitution. Both views are represented at the highest levels, and many leading politicians and officials are themselves unclear about the difference, or undecided over which course to take.

The next step, whatever its motives, was a declaration by the European Council at the Cologne Summit of June 1999, of the need to establish an EU Charter of Fundamental Rights.[3]

THE CHARTER OF FUNDAMENTAL RIGHTS

The resulting Charter contains no rights which are not enjoyed by the citizens of the EU's member states under national law and international agreements such as the Council of Europe's Convention for the Protection of Human Rights and Fundamental Freedoms and the Conventions of the International Labour Organisation. By its own account, the Charter merely establishes the rights which already exist on the basis of the common constitutional traditions and international obligations of the member states. Article 51 of the Charter states specifically that it 'creates no new competences or tasks for the Community or the Union'.

The language of the Charter is often vague to the point of meaninglessness. For example, under Article 38, Consumer Protection, we read that: 'Union policies shall guarantee a high level of consumer protection.' What a 'high level' constitutes is, of course, a matter of opinion. Moreover, the only way consumers can be protected is through strong laws backed up by rigorous enforcement. Such laws exist to one degree or another in all member states. They are backed up by a body of EU consumer protection measures, some of which are useful, especially when it comes to protecting the rights of those buying goods and services outside their own countries. Enforcement is much patchier and more problematic. Article 38 will do nothing to address this problem.

The Charter is full of such pious declarations. Article 25 on the Rights of Older People states that: 'The Union recognises and respects the rights of the elderly to lead a life of dignity and independence and to participate in social and cultural life.' Of course, this is only achievable by those who enjoy a reasonable income, which for almost all retired people means a decent pension. Pensions are entirely in the control of national authorities and the Charter has nothing to say about them.

The essential dishonesty of the whole Charter exercise is revealed whenever any potentially controversial matter is dealt with, in particular anything touching on the rights of employees. Article 27 states that: 'Workers or their representatives must, at the appropriate levels, be guaranteed information and consultation in good time in the cases and under the conditions provided for by Community law and national laws and practices.' This is a statement that is breathtakingly free of content. All it says is that the law must be obeyed, something most people over about four years old are already aware of. In countries where workers have traditionally no right to consultation or information, such as the UK, the article indicates only that national authorities should enforce EU law. Where rights appear to be guaranteed by the Charter, the qualifying phrase is invariably added: the only rights you really have are those guaranteed by national laws and practices.

Such being the case, we are entitled to ask what such an apparently worthless document is actually for. There are two possible answers. Either it is a propaganda exercise to bolster the image of an increasingly unpopular European Union; or it is a deliberate step on the road to a superstate, the seed of a new 'European' constitution. Resistance from numerous member states, including Britain, to any idea that the Charter should be legally binding demonstrated that it is not only those who oppose (or are 'sceptical' of) the European Union who perceive the danger of this. The result, however, is that the precise legal status of the Charter remains unresolved, a battle to be fought at a later date.[4]

THE CITIZEN, JUSTICE, AND HOME AFFAIRS

Maastricht placed earlier informal co-operation in the field of justice and home affairs on a proper legal footing, albeit one which bypassed the institutions of the European Community in favour of a state-to-state approach known as the 'Third Pillar of the European Union'. The Third Pillar applied to nine areas of what was defined as 'common interest'. These were asylum policy, rules governing physical entry to and exit from the Union, immigration, combating drug addiction, fraud on an international scale, judicial co-operation in civil and criminal matters respectively, customs co-operation, and police co-operation to prevent terrorism, drug-trafficking and other serious forms of international crime, this last to include the organisation of a system for exchanging information within a European Police Office to be known as Europol. There was much here to set off civil liberties alarm bells, particularly as the European Parliament was excluded from the decision-making procedure.

In an attempt to respond to this criticism, though the Amsterdam Treaty did not get rid of the three-pillar structure, it did move much of the Third Pillar into the jurisdiction of the EU institutions. What remained were police and judicial co-operation on criminal matters, leaving the planned Europol again outside any visible democratic control.

On the back of these developments the Council and Commission together produced, in 1998, an action plan on the best way to implement Amsterdam's provisions on what the Treaty termed 'the area of freedom, security and justice'. The plan envisaged the incorporation of the Schengen system, an agreement between the majority of member states aimed at establishing freedom of movement between them,[5] into the EU's normal framework, and drew up a timetable regarding free movement of persons, combating trafficking in people and other organised crime, the development of Europol and closer judicial co-operation.

The incorporation of the Schengen system and the general extension of EU powers in the area of civil liberties was widely criticised, above all by people concerned that such democratic control of police and courts as existed in the member states would be weakened or bypassed. Whilst Europol would clearly be under no effective control by national courts, for example, the European Court of Justice was given no powers either to hear individual civil liberties complaints or to exercise any general jurisdiction over the behaviour of police or other law enforcement bodies.

Europol's extensive data-collecting powers include the right to collect information on known and suspected criminals, but also on anyone 'presumed' to be planning to commit a crime and even on potential victims or witnesses, and this data may refer to such irrelevant considerations as racial origin, religious observation, political beliefs, sexuality and health. This 'spooks' charter' is reinforced by the fact that the border-hopping cops' investigative and operational powers appear immune to scrutiny by any democratically elected or otherwise answerable body, whether at national or EU level. The European Parliament is referred to several times in the relevant article of the Amsterdam Treaty, but it is given no power, merely the right to express its views and have them taken into account, hold an annual debate on developments, and ask questions. National Parliaments have only the power to request that their governments issue particular instructions to their representatives on Europol's management board, the body which runs it under the supervision of those governments. Even if the request is respected, however, it can be overruled, as the management board operates on the basis of majority voting.[6]

If the citizens of the EU's member states think they have problems, spare a thought for those people merely resident, or attempting to become so. The Treaties have little to say about the rights of resident non-citizens, but a great deal about control of refugee and asylum policy, as well as immigration in general. Provisions in the Amsterdam Treaty have been criticised not only by left and anti-racist groups, but by Amnesty International, the United Nations High Commission for Refugees (UNHCR), the Quakers and a number of other NGOs about the provisions concerning asylum and refugees. According to these critics, the requirement for unanimity in relation to policy in this area means that policy will inevitably be determined by the member-state government with the most restrictive approach, whilst the Treaty itself violates the convention on refugees which every member state has signed.[7]

Despite the fact that all member states are signatories to the 1951 Geneva Convention on Refugees, the Treaty conflicts with it at a number of points. Its definition of 'refugee', for example, is much narrower, excluding people persecuted by groups not enjoying, or answering to those who enjoy, state power. In an era in which many states have imploded, or when those defined as state authorities may be no more than one of a number of rival groups temporarily in control of the state apparatus, this is clearly an irresponsible erosion of the accepted meaning of the instrument for the international protection of refugees. The Dublin Convention of 1998, an agreement between the member states over implementation of refugee and asylum policy, has met similar criticisms.[8]

Taken together, these various measures clearly demonstrate that the European Union's commitment to 'Fundamental Rights' is not only empty, as can be seen from a simple analysis of the new Charter. It is, in fact, directly contradicted by its actions in the sensitive fields of international policing, asylum and migration. The constant erosion of the powers of democratically elected bodies, the deliberate removal of the security apparatus from any form of popular control, and the blurring of the line between suspicion and guilt, all point to worrying tendencies amongst those who are leading the real, existing process of integration, rather than the one we are constantly assured is bringing us all ever nearer to a borderless, peaceful, internationalist future.

8   The Euro

Whether a nation controls or does not control its own currency is an enormous decision in which democratic values should surely dictate that everyone has the right to participate. Yet even in those countries where a referendum has been held or promised, clear explanations of the advantages and (still more) the disadvantages of such a huge step have been hard to come by, at least from official sources. Instead, the euro has provoked a distilled version of the general pro-EU message: anyone against monetary union is hopelessly mired in the past, viciously nationalistic, sadly out of touch. Those in favour of it are far-sighted, internally-minded, modern.

FOR AND AGAINST

In fact, there is a range of arguments against the euro, emanating from all points on the political compass. There are also arguments in favour of it. Its supporters claim that the EU market will be boosted by the elimination of currency fluctuations, not only getting rid of their associated costs, but allowing industry to plan more easily for the long term. Price differences will become more obvious, increasing consumer power and thus making business more responsive and efficient. Consolidation of European industries will be made easier, and the EU needs industrial and financial giants if it is to compete with the US and Japan. Governments will be forced to create a more business-friendly framework, reforming tax systems and labour markets in a way which, they say, is urgently needed. The euro would be capable of becoming a world currency, rivalling the dollar to the great advantage of EU-based business.

Some of these arguments are valid. The euro certainly carries advantages to business and to individual travellers or people conducting cross-border transactions. How important these will prove is hard to predict, but they are real enough. Alone, however, they will certainly not justify the risk and upheaval involved.

Other arguments are, in fact, identical to those used by opponents. Reforming labour markets is regarded as a good thing by employers understandably concerned to pay the lowest rates of national insurance contributions possible, reduce their tax outlay, and hire and fire at will. For working people who value the stability provided by reliable contracts, decent wages, a functioning system of social security and welfare, and some recognition of their humanity, the benefits of such 'reform' may be hard to fathom.

THE CONVERGENCE CRITERIA

Like the whole of the integrationist project, EMU is politics masquerading as economics. Whatever other motives may lie behind the creation of a single currency or whatever incidental advantages it may have, the euro's primary purpose is to narrow the room for manoeuvre enjoyed by elected governments. As Chancellor Helmut Kohl put it in a speech to the Council of Europe in 1995 'We want the political unification of Europe. If there is no Monetary Union there cannot be Political Union and vice versa.'[1]

The political motivations of the project are evident if we examine the convergence criteria. These are the rules, laid down at Maastricht and incorporated in the Treaty on European Union, which must be followed if a nation wishes its currency to qualify for full membership of EMU. The criteria are as follows:

- Annual average inflation may not exceed by more than 1.5 percentage points the level 'in the three best performing member states in terms of price stability'.
- The level of annual average long-term interest rates may not exceed by more than 2 percentage points the level 'in the three best performing member states in terms of price stability'.
- The government deficit (total public sector) may not exceed 3.0 per cent of gross domestic product (GDP), or should be falling substantially, or be only temporarily above, though still close to, this level.
- Gross government debt may not exceed 60 per cent of GDP, or must show at least a satisfactory reduction towards this figure. A reduction in the debt ratio of 2 per cent of GDP annually would normally be satisfactory.

What is it about these rather dry-sounding criteria which makes the euro such a transparently political project? Quite simply, they are designed to reduce the choices available to member-state governments, so that whatever goals they wish to pursue must be achieved within the confines of a highly liberalised market economy. The real arguments for the euro are the same, then, as the arguments for such an economy, but they are rarely, at least for broad public consumption, presented as such.

Traditionally, national authorities had a wide range of economic and political choice. In democracies, elections are held as a means whereby the people can determine (or at least influence) such choice. Where this is not the case, elections cease to have a great deal of meaning.

Governments have generally responded to economic difficulties, for example, by employing such means as currency devaluation, which can stimulate demand for exports and suppress demand for imports. They can lower interest rates in an attempt to encourage economic activity. They can borrow money and invest it in an economically beneficial way, by improving infrastructure or education, or creating jobs directly.

If none of these things is available, there remains only labour mobility: in good times workers will move in, in bad times they will seek work elsewhere. This, however, simply does not happen in the European Union. People do not cross borders to look for work. Despite the existence of long-standing communities from the Mediterranean in the rich cities of the north, under 1 per cent of the working population of Denmark and Finland, and around 3 per cent in France, Germany and the Netherlands comes from other parts of the EU.

In the United States, on the other hand, a country which is often cited by supporters of the euro as a successful example of a unified currency, the position is very different. Each year, 17 per cent of the population moves house and district. They take with them their pension entitlements, and other benefits, as well as the knowledge that their new neighbours will share their language and much of their cultural baggage. In addition, a large unified federal budget helps to absorb economic shocks. If Texas has economic problems, it can be helped out by transfer of money from a central fund which exists for precisely that purpose. In addition, workers who lose their jobs also stop paying taxes and may become eligible for benefits, thus automatically reducing outflow of wealth from the state. Nothing of this kind exists or is envisaged at the EU's 'federal' level.[2]

Monetary union either abolishes the traditional powers developed by national government or greatly restricts them. In effect, they are handed over to a constitutionally independent, unelected and therefore unaccountable European Central Bank. The question then becomes this: are the advantages of monetary union so great that they justify this loss of democratic control?

WILL THE EURO WORK?

This in turn begs a further question – of whether monetary union under the conditions prevailing in the current European Union will actually work, and, related to this, whether EMU will be capable of being extended to the applicant countries if and when they become part of a greater Union. This is neither a hostile nor a 'sceptical' enquiry. Clearly, a monetary union can work well under some conditions and might be disastrous under others. Where might Euroland, or a Greater Euroland of the near future, fall on this continuum? What, in other words, are the necessary conditions for success?

The first of these is surely popular acceptance and understanding. Whilst downright enthusiasm might be a lot to ask, the affected populations must at the very least be willing to go along with the project, and not simply because virtually the entire political elite supports it and nobody can persuade them to do otherwise. In 2000, popular support, though varying hugely from one member state to another, remained fairly strong. Within the euro-zone it was considerably stronger than it was outside. Overall, 58 per cent of EU inhabitants supported the introduction of the single currency, a slight drop from the previous year, whilst 33 per cent were against it. The euro enjoyed overwhelming support in Italy, Luxembourg, Belgium and Spain: in each of these countries over three-quarters of the population were pro-EMU; this contrasts with only 22 per cent support in the United Kingdom and 38 per cent in Sweden. In Denmark, of course, the population actually had the chance to vote, on 28 September 2000, as to whether they wished to dissolve the Kroner into the euro: they decided, by a narrow majority, to defy the advice of every major political party, trade union and business organisation and retain their own currency.

In most parts of the EU the euro is being introduced with popular acceptance but little enthusiasm. Opposition and scepticism are strongest in those countries which are not participating. Surprisingly, however, support remains relatively weak in Germany, probably because of affection for a Deutsche Mark widely associated with economic recovery and prosperity, whilst a sizeable minority of French people also remains unconvinced.[3]

A second criterion for the success of a monetary union must be a certain convergence between the economies involved. The further apart two economies are in performance, the more difficult it will be to forge a successful union between them. German monetary union following the dissolution of the GDR succeeded, to the degree that it did so, only because Germans from the richer west were willing to invest enormous sums in making it work. Nevertheless, the country experienced severe economic difficulties as a result, whilst the new eastern states suffered, to a great extent, much the same problems as did the other former Communist countries with relatively developed economies – Czechoslovakia, Poland and Hungary.

This is not, however, merely a question of rich and poor. It is also important to know whether economies face similar problems, and if they are likely to face them at more-or-less the same time. In other words, are they at the same point in the economic cycle, and will they continue in step? It is largely the fact that Britain's business cycle is different from that of other EU industrialised countries which has caused Tony Blair's government – which would seem a natural place to look for twelve-starry-eyed fanaticism – to hesitate to take the plunge (though the difficulties of winning the promised referendum have also played their part in this). Britain's differences are a factor of the country's history – and indeed, continuing habit – of doing a great deal of trade outside Europe, including the United States and Japan, whose business cycles are quite different from those of the major EU powers. In addition, Britain produces a significant proportion of her own oil, whilst other EU member states are heavily dependent on imports to meet their energy needs. There are, however, other differences – between those countries which continue to have a major agricultural sector and those which do not, in principal products, and a host of other factors.

Fixing one interest rate for such a wide diversity of economies is bound to cause problems for some member states whilst benefiting others. If Germany and its immediate economic satellites (the Benelux countries) are at the top of their cycle and booming, they will need a quite different rate of interest from that which would help to drag the poorer south of the Union out of a trough. As things stand, this dissonance of cycles can and does occur. The imposition of a single interest rate is comparable to an attempt to control the heating in every house in Europe by means of a thermostat set to respond to the temperature in, say, Frankfurt. In the summer, Cretans would fry whilst Scandinavia shivered. Given the realities of power, interest rates will in reality be fixed to benefit the rich, core economies of the Union.

Again, Britain has particular problems related to monetary union which might lead to opposition to entry from people who have never once waved a Union Jack and who would prefer somebody other than a hereditary head of state to appear on their currency. As individual, private citizens Britons are more directly affected by interest movements than is usual in other parts of the EU. Largely as a result of the fact that houses are bought on mortgages by people further down the economic ladder than would be normal elsewhere, 79 per cent of the country's wealth is tied up in personal debt, as opposed to 24 per cent in Germany and 50 per cent in France. If interest rates rise and you lose your job, you may be unaware of the connection, preferring to believe that it was bad luck, or bad management by your employers. If interest rates rise and your mortgage repayments go up, however, the connection is obvious even to that vast majority of people who find economics less than gripping.[4]

In the end, though, opponents, in common with supporters, must come clean and talk about politics, not economics. Economic and Monetary Union abolishes the right of elected parliaments, governments and institutions directly answerable to them to exercise control over macro-economic policy. It hands it instead to a group of people drawn from the elite of a single profession. This group contains almost no women, no people of colour, no trade unionists, no small business people or farmers. It is constitutionally 'independent' – a positive-sounding word which is always used to describe the European Central Bank but for some reason rarely applied to other dictatorships. Whatever economic advantages it may or may not have, the single currency as prescribed in the Maastricht Treaty has, in one extremely clever stroke, abolished the tiresome influence of popular, democratic institutions on macro-economic policy, a matter now far too important for anything so frivolous to be allowed to intrude.[5]

Box 8.1

The Stages of Monetary Union

First stage (1 July 1990–31 December 1993)

- Completion of the internal market by end of 1992 (see Chapter 9).
- Strengthening of economic co-ordination.

Second stage (1 January 1994–31 December 1998)

- Establishment of European Monetary Institute (EMI) to assist member states in co-ordinating policies, prepare third stage of EMU, in particular the establishment of the European System of Central Banks (ESCB), and to oversee the development of the European Currency Unit (ECU), the notional currency which preceded the euro to oversee the development of the ECU.

- Member states obliged to
  - render their central banks independent of the political authorities;
  - discontinue their overdraft facilities with their central banks and their privileged access to financial institutions;
  - endeavour to fulfil the following five convergence criteria:

  1. An average rate of inflation that does not exceed by more than 1.5 percentage points that of the three best-performing Member States during the year preceding the third stage.
  2. A budgetary deficit not exceeding 3 per cent of GDP, or close to that level, provided that it has declined continuously.
  3. Government debt not exceeding 60 per cent of GDP, or close to that level owing to a sharply diminishing trend.
  4. A long-term interest rate that does not exceed by more than 2 per cent the average of the three best-performing member states in terms of price stability.
  5. Maintenance of the national currency within the normal fluctuation margins of the European Monetary System for at least two years, without devaluation.

- The European Council has the right to set date for passage to the third stage, though with a minimum date and cut-off date. In the event the Madrid European Council of December 1995 decided that the third stage would begin on 1 January 1999 and that the decision as to the participating member states would be taken as soon as possible in 1998.

- The participating nations were named as Austria, Belgium, Germany, Luxembourg, the Netherlands, Spain, Portugal, Italy, Ireland, France, and Finland.

Third stage (1 January 1999–1 July 2002 at the latest)

- Establishment of the European System of Central Banks (ESCB) and the European Central Bank (ECB).
- Introduction of the euro.

On 1 January 1999

- The parities of the participating currencies and their rates of conversion into euros irrevocably fixed; the amounts expressed in national currencies in contracts converted into euros.
- The euro became a currency in its own right (but no coins or notes issued until 1 January 2002).
- Member states' monetary policy and exchange-rate policy carried out, and new public-sector debt instruments issued, in euros.
- ESCB and national and Community public authorities to oversee and assist with changeover.
- By 1 January 2002 at the latest, euro banknotes and coins to circulate alongside national currency notes and coins.
- By July 2002 at the latest, national currency banknotes and coins to be withdrawn and only euro banknotes and coins to be legal tender.

- Co-ordination of economic policies according to following system: the Council of Ministers lays down the broad guidelines of the economic policies of the member states and of the Community after reporting to the European Council and taking account of its conclusions. The Council then ensures compliance with these broad guidelines and monitors economic developments in the member states. It monitors excessive public deficits, and, after the Commission has issued its Opinion, the Council of Ministers decides whether a member state has such a deficit and recommends measures to be taken by that member state with a view to eliminating it within a specified time-limit. Should the member state fail to adopt such measures, the Council may decide to impose sanctions.

Stability and growth pact maintain budgetary discipline indefinitely

- by requiring member states participating in monetary union to draw up and submit stability programmes to maintain medium-term budgetary equilibrium,
- by laying down the timetable for implementation, and sanctions under the excessive deficits procedure.

Box 8.2

Who's in Charge of the Euro?

The European Central Bank (ECB) (est. July 1998).

- Directed by an Executive Board comprising a President, Vice-President and two to four other members, all appointed by the EMU member state governments for a non-renewable period of eight years. The Executive Board is responsible for the daily management of the ECB and, in particular, for the implementation of monetary policy on the basis of the decisions of the Governing Council.
- The Governing Council consists of the President and Vice-President of the Executive Board and the Governors of the Central Banks of the EMU member countries. It defines monetary policy and establishes the necessary guidelines for its implementation. It is thus the ECB's supreme decision-making body.
- A General Council consisting of the President and Vice-President of the ECB and the Governors of the Central Banks of all the member states of the European Union; prepares for the possible accession of EU member states not already members of the euro-zone.

The ECB has the following tasks:

- To administer the European System of Central Banks.
- To address an annual report on the activities of the ESCB and the monetary policy of both the previous and the current year to the Council, Parliament and Commission.

The European System of Central Banks (ESCB) (est. 1 July 1998) consists of the ECB and the national central banks. It is governed by the decision-making bodies of the ECB and has the following tasks, all of which are carried out with a view to its fundamental responsibility, to maintain price stability:

- To define and implement the single monetary policy.
- To conduct foreign-exchange operations arising from the exchange-rate policy established by the Council.
- To hold and manage the foreign reserves of the participating member states.
- To ensure the smooth operation of payment systems in the euro area.
- To contribute to the smooth conduct of policies relating to the stability of the financial system.
- To authorise the issue of banknotes in the euro area.

The Economic and Financial Committee has six members, two appointed by the member states, two by the Commission and two by the ECB. Took over most of the functions of the Monetary Committee, which it succeeded on 1 January 1999.

The Euro Council co-ordinates economic policies in the euro-zone. Cannot take decisions independently, however. They must be confirmed by the EU Economic and Financial Affairs Council (Ecofin) in accordance with the usual procedures laid down in the Treaties.

9   The Internal Market

Whatever its longer-term political objectives may have been, the immediate goal of the 1957 Treaty of Rome was the establishment of a single, or 'common' market. To that end, the Treaty established deadlines for the removal of customs duties or tariffs. This process was successfully concluded well within the allotted time. By the late 1960s, with very rare exceptions, anything made in one of the Six could be exported to another member state without duty having to be paid. Member states were also banned from excluding, or placing quantitative restrictions on, imports of products from other member states, unless they could show that the goods were a threat to public health, order or morals, the exceptions specifically allowed by the Treaty of Rome. Why, then, did the Commission feel it necessary to publish, in 1985, a white paper 'on completing the internal market'?[1]

The answer lies in the murky area of 'barriers to trade'. If you want to create a single market, the simple removal of obvious barriers to trade such as tariffs or duties on imports is only the beginning. You must then convince or force national authorities not to use, for example, laws designed to protect the consumer or the environment in a mischievous way, excluding foreign imports which, though in reality perfectly safe and reliable, do not happen to conform to the precise description contained in your code of laws. As member states rapidly removed tariffs and duties, they tended to take advantage of the potential of such things as technical specifications to exclude foreign competition (or at least place it at a disadvantage) as well as on some occasions giving a somewhat loose interpretation of those exceptions to free trade allowed by the Treaty.

VITAL REGULATION OR 'BARRIER TO TRADE'?

This, however, is to look at the matter in a one-sided way – the way in which enthusiasts for a single market tend to look at it. Anyone who has followed the recent history of the World Trade Organisation (WTO) and opposition to it will understand that there is often another side to the story.

Like the WTO, the EU ostensibly attempts to establish fair trade between nations. Just as in the case of the WTO, this involves not only removing duties, but attacking anything and everything which can be seen as an example of a government or other national authority giving an unfair advantage to its own producers over those from other countries. Environmental regulations, consumer protection laws, rules to promote public health or the safety of workers, can all result in the exclusion of particular foreign imports and all can therefore be declared illegal. The only difference on this level between the EU and the WTO is that the EU has far more extensive power and involves a much greater handing-over of decision-making from national institutions to supra-national bodies.

Two important rulings by the European Court of Justice illustrate the potential conflict between environmental protection or consumers' interest (to take just two examples) and the drive to remove trade barriers. Both involved booze, and both helped lay the foundations of internal market case law. In the first, the *Cassis de Dijon* case of 1979 concerned a German law which prevented this French beverage being sold over the border because its self-description as a 'liqueur' did not conform to the German definition. The ECJ ruled that this was an unacceptable interference with trade, establishing the principle that, with the exceptions mentioned above, a product which could legally be sold in one member state could legally be sold in all of them. In the second, in 1987, Germany was forced to accept the import of beers which contained additives forbidden under the national law, which has strict rules on 'purity' dating back to the sixteenth century. This latter case was more worrying to consumer advocates, as it could be viewed as forcing one member state to lower its standards to those which prevailed in others, a problem to which opponents of the EU (as well as anti-WTO activists) like to draw attention. The ECJ does not, however, always take the side of the 'single market'. From time to time it has upheld alleged barriers to trade in the face of legal challenges, for example allowing Denmark to continue to insist that drinks be sold in returnable bottles.[2]

The elimination of hidden barriers to trade prevents countries from placing their firms' foreign competitors at a disadvantage. But what about the opposite approach? What if a government wants – perhaps in order to preserve jobs in an area of high unemployment, or tide a company through a sticky patch – to give a helping hand to an enterprise in its own country?

The answer is that it may do so, but only under very strict conditions and with the permission of the European Commission. Powers to regulate state aid are classed as part of competition policy. The Treaty of Rome prohibits any form of state aid that is likely to distort intra-Community competition, on the grounds that it is incompatible with the common market. 'State' aid includes that which might be given by a local authority or any other body which distributes public money. As well as straightforward grants or financial awards, this covers soft loans (i.e. those given at favourable rates of interest or other conditions), loan guarantees, tax breaks, the supply of goods or services on preferential terms, and the use of any sort of public ownership or part-ownership to gain an advantage. Exemptions are allowed for aid having a (strictly interpreted and narrowly defined) social character, or to make good the damage caused by exceptional events such as natural disasters. In addition, assistance is sometimes allowed to aid underdeveloped regions, to promote the execution of a major project of European interest or remedy a serious disturbance in the economy of a member state, to facilitate the development of certain economic activities or areas or to promote culture and heritage conservation (with the same proviso), and, exceptionally, for anything to which the Council gives its assent.

COMPETITION POLICY

These rules on state aid are part of a broader approach known as 'competition policy'. Competition policy is the glue that holds the single market together. The Treaty of Rome forbids measures 'which may affect trade between Member States and which have as their object or effect the prevention, restriction of distortion of competition within the common market' (Art.81). The details laid out in the Treaty, and the body of law generated since, are therefore directed against three targets: concerted practices (where firms make secret deals, for example to avoid price competition); abuse of a dominant position in the market for a particular good or service; and use of state aid to enable a firm or industry to gain an 'unfair' advantage over rivals in another member state. Exemptions are allowed in certain instances, where it is felt that an arguably anti-competitive practice is in the long-term interest of 'the market' or of the economic wellbeing of the Union as a whole. For example, firms are not permitted to co-operate in order to limit production or carve up markets, but they may do so to promote technical progress. The rules are policed by the Commission, which has the power to investigate cases, issue exemptions or bring abuses to an end, and levy fines. The Commission sometimes even stages 'Untouchables'-style dawn raids which does its staid, overfed image no harm at all. In addition, the Commission may investigate company mergers likely to create dominant market positions affecting trade between member states, may order mergers not to go ahead or particular aspects of them to cease, and impose fines.

THE SINGLE EUROPEAN ACT

The Commission's 1985 white paper on the internal market laid the basis for the so-called Single European Act (SEA), a series of amendments to the Treaty of Rome which came into force on 1 July 1987.[3] The major institutional change introduced by the SEA was the extension of majority voting, which had previously been quite restricted in use, to certain well-defined policy areas – generally those concerning the completion of the internal market. The argument for this is that it makes decision-making quicker and more 'efficient'. The argument against is that it immediately undermines the power of the electorate – because one's own government can be outvoted by foreign authorities over which one has no control, and thus be unable to put into practice the policies on which it fought the election.

Politicians are hardly famous for keeping their promises. QMV, however, can make it literally impossible for them to do so. The SEA did, it's true, increase the powers of the European Parliament; but even if one accepts that the EP can indeed be a substitute for nationally-based elected institutions (which, as we have seen, is itself problematic), it was hardly given the weight it would need to control the Council of Ministers in the way that a national parliament can, under the constitutions of most member states, monitor a government's behaviour.

This brings us, in fact, to the most important argument against this European Union. To understand this, we need to look at the full implications of 'single internal market without barriers to trade' and why this makes a particular version of the 'free market' or of 'capitalism', compulsory.

This is not to say that the whole single-market process is bogus, or simply a way of imposing a particular system on electorates which for the most part have assumed that the existence of parties of right and left gave them a choice of social and economic systems, and not merely faces, ties and smiles. The removal of technical barriers to trade is clearly a process that offers different national producers mutual advantages, because the existence of a single set of technical specifications reduces the cost of research, development, manufacture and marketing.

Problems appear when you begin to argue about standards. Progressive supporters of the EU have always argued for the highest existing standards and best current practices to be generalised. If one member state does it best, everyone should copy them. Against this idea, however, is invariably a huge lobbying effort from the industries who would be obliged to respond to greater restrictions. The highest standard, decision-makers at the Commission, Parliament, Council and in the national governments are invariably told, is over-restrictive, would be expensive to implement and (this is always the big one) would 'cost jobs'.

WIDOWS, ORPHANS AND JOBS

In nineteenth-century America there was a tendency for those who opposed any and all restrictions on the developing capitalist economy to claim that their only real concern was with the small investments of 'widows and orphans'. These unfortunate bereaved souls were wheeled out by politicians and industrialists who were not otherwise noted for their concern for social solidarity. The modern equivalent is the magic word 'jobs', the protection of which for some reason appears to demand ever-lower social and environmental standards.

The result of the vigorous activities of hugely rich corporations and their highly-paid and multitudinous lobbyists is usually presented as a compromise between 'extremes', but it is almost (though not quite) always one which favours not the best existing practice but, on the contrary, the lowest common denominator. The respective power of, on the one hand, the lobby of financiers, industrialists, agribusiness, food processors and so on, and, on the other, consumer protection lobbies, trade unionists, environmentalist or public health groups and their sympathisers in left and green political parties, of course massively favours the former. This is true at national level, but the costs and difficulties of lobbying in Strasbourg are that much greater, increasing the advantage enjoyed by those with money and power. The result is that the only real exceptions to the lowest common denominator rule tend to result from crises (such as the BSE scandal) or to come when the interests of the richest countries and manufacturers appear to coincide with those of the consumer. This is what happened, for instance, in the case of the acceptance of catalytic converters by car manufacturers, who knew well enough that much more effective and expensive solutions to air pollution were needed, and saw the attachment of a reassuring-sounding gizmo to the exhaust system of cars as a way of staving off pressure in favour of something much more inimical to their profits.[4]

FOUR FREEDOMS: SOME FREER THAN OTHERS

The single internal market's implications do not, moreover, stop there. An internal market is supposed to be based on what have been called the 'four freedoms': movement of goods, capital, services and labour. The last of these has caused the EU more headaches than almost any other subject, and the general reason for this is that although the 'free market' system insists on regarding labour as a commodity, it is of course no such thing. Labour is a direct human activity which requires the presence of the sentient being involved. He or she, despite the inconvenience caused to the system by these phenomena, continues to have many needs, desires, aspirations, thoughts, feelings, interests, problems and pastimes which do not contribute to the productive process. This has always made the idea of the free movement of labour a complex issue.

The Treaty of Rome gave 'workers' (its own word) the right to move freely within the territory of the European Economic Community's member states, but only in order to seek or carry out employment. The right to reside was conditional on the migrant's having employment, although, having been employed, a person had the right to remain in the country where he or she worked. Employers may not discriminate between nationals of different member states, in relation to hiring, pay or conditions. The right to reside after employment ends is in practice limited by the fact that states *may* discriminate when it comes to welfare systems.

Generally speaking, the contributory element of any system must be non-discriminatory. If you have worked and paid into a scheme for unemployment insurance, sickness benefits, state retirement pensions and so on, then you are entitled to benefit, whether or not you are a citizen of the country in which you worked. You are not, however, entitled to non-contributory welfare payments, those which do not depend on a person's having worked and paid into a scheme.

To take an example, in all countries of the EU15 a state pension scheme exists to which employed people make contributions in proportion to their salaries. At the legal age of retirement, a calculation is made which determines the level of your pension. Usually, this will be influenced by how many years you have worked, and, in some cases, by the level of your earnings. In most countries, a full state pension, perhaps with an earnings-related element, is at least adequate to cover the basics of life.

At the same time, numerous people who, for one reason or another, have not been in paid employment for a substantial part of their lives, will either not qualify for a pension or will be paid at a reduced level. Generally, these people are not allowed to starve in the street or even thrown completely on to the mercy of family or charity, although the pressure for pension 'reform' may well lead to a return to such conditions. Usually, people will have whatever pension to which they are entitled topped up to some notional minimum income, through various maintenance, housing or other benefits, none of which depend on any contributions having been made. This is what is often termed the 'safety net', and in this element state authorities are with few exceptions allowed to limit payments to their own citizens.

Other rights enjoyed by EU migrant workers include 'aggregation', through which pension rights accumulated in one country may be added to those gathered in another, so that if you work for 20 years in one country and 20 in another, you will be treated, with certain provisos, as if you have worked for 40 years in the same place. In addition, persons seeking work in another member state are entitled, for a maximum of three months, to receive benefits from their last country of employment. Finally, child benefits and family allowances, though non-contributory, must be paid to migrants. Close family members of migrant workers also derive certain rights from the employment of their, for example, husband, wife or parent.

The question of welfare rights, though problematic, is probably not the place to look for an explanation of why trans-frontier labour migration is close to non-existent within the EU. People's willingness to move to seek or take up employment elsewhere is in practice limited by numerous factors. Such willingness is confined almost exclusively to specific groups: young people intending to see something of the world before they begin a career; a small number who are simply footloose, adventurous or on the run from the law or worse; the highly educated; and, finally, the desperate. Most people who leave their home countries – or even their home regions – in order to find work do so because they have no choice. Many are men who move without their families, sending most of their pay home to Portugal, Turkey, or Teesside.

This is not the case everywhere in the world. The biggest and best-known exception is the United States, which has a single common language, has been a single market for over two centuries, and has a culture which contains a large element of the homogenous: laws and customs, food and drink, systems of housing and education and so on, do differ between states and regions, but there is always a core which does not vary, and a narrow band of differences – often enough to allow for regional pride, and to make a new place interesting, but not threatening or bewildering. The achievement of such a degree of cultural unification would require changes in European society which would make it as unrecognisable to us as we would be to ancient Romans. 'Globalisation' notwithstanding, it is unlikely to happen in a thousand years and, without it, labour mobility will continue to be confined to the above-listed groups.

Mutual recognition of educational and vocational qualifications, the rights of self-employed people and the freedom to provide services are other issues which have to be tackled on the road to the achievement of free movement, and in each case the legislative situation has been greatly reformed since the original Treaty was signed. The situation on the ground, however, can be quite different from that which exists on paper. It is all too easy for an obstructive authority, or even an individual bureaucrat, to erect barriers to the establishment of a business, to question unfamiliar qualifications, to discriminate in favour of local providers of services. Such behaviour may be motivated by xenophobia, but it can equally well be directed at the preservation of valued local customs and traditions. Whatever the motivation, however, it can be extremely successful in making it impossible for foreigners to take advantage of rights contained in treaties and regulations.

CAPITAL

Capital, unlike labour, enjoys complete freedom of movement and rarely encounters obstruction or prejudice when it arrives at its destination. A Directive of 1988 guarantees the full liberalisation of all capital movements.[5] EMU has, of course, facilitated these movements. Whether such freedom stimulates economic activity is a question which is never posed in the mainstream media. A case can certainly be made for the opposite view. The fact that it makes big corporations far more difficult to tax is, however, unquestionable.

PRIVATE GOOD, PUBLIC BAD

The phase of integration which followed the beginning of Phase 1 of the EMU process included an attempt to develop the infrastructure necessary to promote the single market as a physical reality. There is not much value in having the right to sell your Aberdeen kippers in Athens if you can't get them there, and for that you need better railways, roads, inland waterways and so on, or so it is argued. And so was born the idea of Trans European Networks (TENs).

Under TENs, motorways are built in the name of 'relieving congestion' despite extensive evidence that they are completely ineffective in doing so. Aid to rail promotes high-speed trains which, though admittedly an enjoyable way of getting around Western Europe for those who can afford it, do nothing to tackle the real problem of a declining rail network, despite the European Commission's constant lip-service to the environmental advantages of rail over road.

In telecommunications, the emphasis has been on the creation of so-called 'information highways', particularly regarding electronic systems which directly facilitate the running of the internal market, but this has been conducted in parallel with huge pressure to liberalise as a supposed pre-condition of the modernisation of services. TENs in the energy sector aim at the integration of increasingly liberalised gas and electricity sectors, though other targets are to underwrite European firms' international competitiveness by supplying them with relatively cheap (as well as reliable) energy, an aim which is clearly approved by corporate capital but which does not always sit easily with environmental objectives or with the interests of the ordinary domestic consumer. TENs have also been directed at the integration of waste management policy and water delivery. TENs projects are financed from the Cohesion Fund, from the European Investment Bank and from private capital, sometimes in the form of loans guaranteed through the European Investment Fund.

The drive to complete the single internal market also saw the introduction, more or less by stealth, of an assumption into the commandments of Political Correctness by which the EU is ruled: private enterprise good, public enterprise bad. Nowhere in the Treaties does it say that the state must withdraw from economic life. Numerous details, particularly of competition policy, can, however, be interpreted to mean just that. When publicly owned enterprises are forbidden to use the advantages of public ownership to compete with private firms – for example, the ability to transfer wealth from more productive to less productive economic activities in the interests of the general good, rather than shareholders' profits – they cease to function in the way that was envisaged by their instigators. Nationalised industries can no doubt be just as ruthless and therefore just as profitable as any private firm, but then what precisely is the point of them?

The fact is that publicly owned undertakings are an embarrassment to the Treaty of Rome. This is because market distortion is generally the whole point of social ownership. For example, buses may be municipally owned in order to 'distort' a market which, were it allowed to function 'freely', would force people to walk everywhere; health care is usually publicly funded in order to 'distort' the natural consequences of the market, which in this case would be to allow large numbers of people to suffer and die for want of funds. The Treaty of Rome does not forbid public ownership; it is simply that, strictly interpreted, it outlaws the practices which make it advantageous. Public enterprises may not be granted privileges which give them an advantage over potential competitors in other member states: Austria's state-owned monopoly of import and wholesaling of alcoholic drinks was abolished when the country joined the Union, for example. Two special categories of undertaking – those responsible for a fiscal monopoly, and those providing a service of general economic interest may be given privileges which would normally contradict the Treaty of Rome, provided any such exemption is necessitated by the particular tasks assigned to the undertaking and does not disrupt trade to an extent that would be contrary to the Community's interests. Yet the qualifying rules for such an exemption are vague and shifting: in postal services, for example, the space reserved for the public service is subject to progressive reduction. The problem this approach causes is known as 'cherry picking': private firms get all the lucrative business whilst the taxpayer is left to ensure that sheep farmers and lighthouse keepers continue to get Christmas cards from their mums.

The single internal market project can be said to have been, in its own terms, a success. It has created a market of some 375 million people in 18 countries, as not only the EU15 but the three small countries which remain in the European Free Trade Association – Norway, Iceland and Lichtenstein – also participate, through a system known as the European Economic Area. Its supporters argue that it has succeeded in reducing the cost of manufacture and transport of goods, though by how much is disputed and difficult to specify. The big market, furthermore, is said to increase 'Europe's' economic weight and thus its political clout.

MIXED BLESSINGS

Many of the alleged benefits of the single market are, like most things, good in some ways, perhaps, but damaging or otherwise undesirable in others. Cheaper transport, for example, (which may in any case have more to do with a decade of relatively low oil prices coupled with a sustained, vicious and hugely successful assault on transport workers' pay and conditions) is hardly an unquestionable boon. Whilst it may have appeared to increase the variety and lowered the price of goods available to the consumer, to the extent that this has been achieved it has been at the cost of enormous environmental damage. The transport of goods is now so cheap that costs, in terms of their contribution to prices, have become less and less significant. The result is that it is possible to buy Swedish or Welsh mineral water in Belgium, a country whose normal weather is rain. French apples travel to Italy and Italian apples to France. Variety is not increased, because the range of fruit grown in any particular country or region becomes ever narrower. In a similar way, as transport costs lower, freight traffic is shifted from rail to road and new motorways spring up to disfigure the landscape, jobs naturally cluster in booming urban centres at the expense of 'less favoured regions'.

Removal of frontiers to the movement of capital and goods has also encouraged delocalisation, the movement of productive facilities from higher to lower cost countries. This in turn puts downward pressure on those things which benefit the rest of us but cost corporate profits: wages, social standards, health and safety regulations, environmental controls. Like the WTO, moreover, the European Union, with its enforcement powers through the Commission and Court of Justice, makes it more difficult for national authorities to take action in defence of these.

As with so many things, the balance sheet of costs and benefits arising from the single market tends to depend on who you are. For big corporations the benefits are clear. For the rest of us the picture is at best much more mixed. Many of what might seem the obvious pluses of a single labour market have turned out to be rather more problematic than we were told would be the case, especially when it comes to enforcement of rights. The free movement of goods has some benefits, but also great costs to the environment as well as to small producers and distributors. It is hard to see how free movement of capital benefits the mass of people who do not own any, and the fact that banks maintain outrageously high charges for people who wish to move small amounts of money between countries tells its own story.

CONSUMER PROTECTION

As we have seen, the Treaty of Rome was principally concerned with people as economic actors – employers, workers, etc. – rather than as citizens. This did not rule out competence for consumer policy, however, as buying goods and services is as much an economic act as producing them. Nevertheless, little attention was paid to the matter before the first EC Consumer Action Programme began in 1975. In fact, only since Amsterdam has the EU paid close attention to what the Treaty (Article 153) describes as the Community's duty to 'contribute to protecting the health, safety and economic interests of consumers as well as to promoting their right to information, education and to organise themselves in order to safeguard their interests'.[6]

Other requirements laid down in the Treaty include the stronger integration of consumer interests into other policies and the taking into account of scientific evidence in the evaluation of proposals concerning health, safety, environmental protection and consumer protection measures. Individual member states are specifically authorised by the Treaty to take more stringent measures than those agreed at EU level, providing they do not conflict in other ways with the Treaty. The aims of EU consumer policy are given as enabling the consumer to exercise his or her rights to protection of health and safety, financial and legal interests, and to representation, participation, information and education. Initiatives guided by these principles have concentrated on informing the consumer so that he or she can make an educated choice, and protecting health and safety.

The most recent Action Plan, Priorities for Consumer Policy 1996–1998 (COM(95)0519) was based on these priorities, with particular reference to the developing single market, to financial services, essential public services, new telecommunications technologies (the 'Information Society'), and food. The Action Plan also concerned itself with environmental questions ('sustainable consumption'), consumer representation, consumers in the applicant states of Central and Eastern Europe and in developing countries.

Major EU measures in favour of the consumer include the 1992 General Product Safety Directive, a series of directives restricting the marketing and use of dangerous substances, countless food safety laws, and rules governing cosmetics, toys, and medicines. In the wake of the ongoing BSE crisis, as well as scares over dioxins, e-coli, salmonella, pesticide residues and GMOs, particular attention is now being paid to food. During the 1990s, directives were also agreed on consumer redress, liability for defective products, and unfair terms in contracts. Also governed or affected by EU legislation are door-to-door sales, distance selling, consumer credit, time share and package holidays, airline fares and overbooking, misleading advertising and price indication. Famous abuses which the EU authorities have failed to deal with include the fact that cars are distributed under a monopolistic system which is mysteriously allowed to ignore all of the normal rules of competition policy and which results in price differentials between member states of up to 40 per cent, and they are increasing. Volkswagen has actually been fined (102m ECUs, in 1998) by the Commission for systematically preventing its Italian dealers from selling VW and Audi cars to non-Italian clients – mostly

Germans who crossed the border to save thousands of marks by buying a German car in Italy, a difficult one to call for those who believe in patriotic shopping. Rip-offs associated with cross-border payments have also proved stubborn, with the Commission perhaps waiting until the magic wand of the euro waves the problem away. A Community System for the Exchange of Information aids communication between member states on dangerous products.

10   External Economic Relations

The creation of a customs union in 1968 removed a number of remaining restrictions on the internal market. It also established a common external tariff as part of a common commercial policy governing trade relations between the Community and the rest of the world. The aim was to reduce destructive competition between member states, as well as to ensure that once goods had been imported, they could move around the EC as freely as could those manufactured within it.

External trade has long given the European Commission its highest profile on the world stage. Because of the existence of the customs union and since it affects external trade, the EC, then EU, has had to be represented in its own right at trade negotiations with Third Countries (EU jargon for any country not a member of the Union). Indeed, with regard to agriculture and fisheries the member states play very little direct part in negotiations. A set of guidelines and goals is agreed by the Council, which then communicates this to the Commission, after which the Commission gets on with it. In other areas, where responsibility for policy remains to a great extent with the individual member states, national negotiators are obliged to respect a ruling of the ECJ in determining their stance.

IMPORTS

The most important element of the EU's trade policy remains the Common Customs Tariff (CCT). This Tariff must of course be agreed between 15 member states with sometimes diverse and conflicting interests, but it must also be negotiated with international trading partners in the context, originally, of the General Agreement on Tariffs and Trade (GATT), and now of the World Trade Organisation (WTO).

In addition to the CCT, imports are governed by a set of common rules applying to all products from outside the EU, with a special system governing textiles, which are subject (world-wide) to quotas and special rules. Products originating from certain countries may also be subject to special restrictions for political reasons, of course.

In recent times the EU has taken part in trade embargoes against, or placed other forms of restriction on *inter alia*, Iraq, Libya, Yugoslavia, Myanmar (Burma), China, the USA and Canada.

Finally, special arrangements govern the import of various farm products. These are usually hangovers from agreements which predate the Treaty of Rome and have their roots in colonial systems or those negotiated when former colonies became independent. Preferential treatment may therefore be exercised, ostensibly at least to prevent the collapse of economies dependent for historical reasons on trade with one or more EU member states. This occurs particularly under the ACP system (the initials stand simply for Africa, Caribbean, Pacific) which for the most part embraces the member states' former imperial possessions. This can be controversial, as was the case in the long-running dispute between the EU and the US over bananas.[1]

If member states believe that they have been subject by a particular Third Country to unfair trading practices – such as the dumping of goods for below cost price, which is sometimes done to cut losses, or with the deliberate intention of harming a rival national industry – they cannot act independently, but must bring the matter to the attention of the Commission, which investigates. This may result in what is officially known as 'surveillance', including 'retrospective surveillance' covering the recent history of imports of the commodity or commodities involved from the alleged offending country. Action may include the imposition of anti-dumping duties, though the Third Country involved can contest the validity of these by taking its case to the WTO. Other than straightforward dumping, both the EU and WTO allow protective measures to be taken in cases of exports from Third Countries where the products in question have been made cheaper by state subsidies, in which case a countervailing duty can be imposed to offset the price reduction brought about by the subsidy.

Clearly, the same problems exist in relation to these rules on external imports as is the case with the internal market. As far as trading partners are concerned, policy choices are narrowed by the ban on state aid. Member states may also be prevented from imposing quotas or bans in response to demands from their own citizens, or parliaments. Environmentally damaging products, or those from firms or countries which are exploitative (for example, using child labour, or refusing workers the right to organise), can be subject to restrictions only if these are agreed by the rest of the EU.

On the other hand, trade embargoes such as that imposed on Iraq after the Gulf War cannot be unilaterally lifted by a member state which may have decided the time has come to do so. The perceived danger is that, in common with the WTO, the European Commission is likely always to bow to the most powerful pressures. Occasionally this may be public opinion, but it is far more likely to be the commercial needs of big corporations.

EXPORTS

As well as the CCT and other measures governing imports, the Community operates a common set of arrangements on exports. Exports may not in general be subject to quantitative limits, though exceptions are allowed. Major exceptions are petrol and natural gas, trade in which is sensitive and regulated by a complex system of international agreements.

Normally, if a member state believes that market conditions are such that limiting the amount of a commodity which can be exported would be justified, it must ask the Commission to initiate what is known as a 'Community information and consultation procedure'. Equally, the Commission may decide to do this on its own initiative. If the Commission concludes that extraordinary measures are justified, it can make exports subject to special authorisation. Such authorisations may apply to a commodity or group of commodities, either from the whole of the EU or a region or country, and may also be limited to particular destinations. Any proposed action by the Commission must then be approved by the Council.

Any measure taken by a member state to stimulate exports must, insofar as it constitutes a state aid, be approved by the Commission. Obviously, if one member state were to give aid to exporters of a particular commodity, this might give its own national producers what the EU and its treaties see as an unfair advantage. The general approach has not, however, been to attempt to eradicate such aid but to harmonise systems in pursuit of that mythical grail, the level playing field. There is also some EU-level assistance to exporters, but outside of the special case of the Common Agricultural Policy this is generally limited to providing finance for joint action and research, including events such as trade fairs and seminars.

The EU does not, of course, devise its trade policies independently. Since 1947, international trade has been governed by multilateral institutions, the most important of which, for the western, capitalist world, was originally the General Agreement on Trade and Tariffs (GATT), which, after the collapse of the alternative trade system dominated by the Soviet Union, gave birth to the World Trade Organisation (WTO).

The GATT/WTO philosophy is 'free trade good, protection bad'. As this is also the driving philosophy behind the EEC/EC/EU integrationist project, one would expect the Community/Union to be amongst the GATT/WTO's best pupils. This has not, in fact, always been the case, as the temptation for the Union, a temptation which has grown with its territory, is to pursue the alternative – the creation of a self-sufficient market behind impenetrable external borders. Within the context of the Common Agricultural Policy, and here and there in other spheres as well, the European Union continues, when it suits it, to use protectionist devices. This hypocrisy, however, should not blind us to the facts: the Union has been a major driving force behind the liberalisation of world trade, and there seems little prospect of this changing. Taken as a bloc, the EU is the world's biggest trader.[2]

GLOBALISATION

'Free trade' has become the dominant economic philosophy of global capitalism and is now broadly interpreted to imply wholesale deregulation, liberalisation, privatisation and the imposition of institutionalised external pressures (Structural Adjustment Programmes for the Third World, the EMU convergence criteria for the European Union) which have led to the dismantling of welfare states, to wage cuts, delocalisation of production and even (the case of Yugoslavia is the best documented) to war.

What began as an economic project, the 'freeing' of trade, has become a crusade which, like the EU itself, reaches into every corner of life. The logic which led from the Common Market to the Single European Market, to the single currency and beyond, works in the same way at the global level.

This is the meaning of 'anti-globalisation', the solution to the apparent paradox of why the most internationally-minded people see globalisation as a threat. Globalisation, like 'Europe', is not a politically and economically neutral phenomenon which simply transfers the same arguments – between market economies and mixed economies, for example, or between the 'social market' and socialism – to new fora at new levels of international debate and co-operation. Both are, on the contrary, quite clearly attempts to abolish these debates, to negate or ignore the contradictions which give rise to them, and to take decision-making ever further from the people into remote bodies which, moreover, do not admit to taking decisions at all. Instead, they follow inevitabilities created by mysterious 'market forces', the invisible hand strangling the life from any alternative which may remain.

DEVELOPMENT POLICY

Until Maastricht, the European Community could not point to anything in the Treaty of Rome which specifically gave it competence in the area of development policy. Nevertheless, it was able to pursue a limited agenda through the Lomé Convention, an agreement with countries known as the ACP (Africa, Caribbean, Pacific) group, mainly ex-colonies of France, Britain, Portugal, Belgium and the Netherlands which enjoyed preferential access to European Community markets. The EC was also party to various Association Agreements with developing nations and to numerous other trade agreements with a development element.[3]

New Articles added at Maastricht put the policy on a firmer legal footing, giving it four principal objectives: to promote sustainable economic and social development, with special attention to the very poorest countries; integration of developing countries into the world economy; reduction of poverty; and consolidation of democracy, the rule of law and respect for human rights. The implementation of the resulting policy is carried out partly through regional agreements, of which Lomé is only one. In addition, the EU has agreements with countries of two regions of the Near and Middle East, covering Algeria, Tunisia and Morocco on the one hand and Egypt, Jordan, Syria and Lebanon on the other.

The Union is also, of course, involved in a large number of inter-national agreements and conventions with development implications: the World Trade Organisation, various nature conser-vation and other environmental treaties, and so on. In addition, it has formalised trade relations and agreements on financial and technical aid with several developing countries and trade blocs in Latin America (where the trade bloc is known as Mercosur) and Asia

(ASEAN). Finally, the EU is empowered by its Treaties to offer humanitarian aid and administers a special fund to combat world hunger.

The Commission, which is responsible for the day-to-day administration of development and trade policies, sees aid as a 'lever for economic and political reform'. This in turn implies that policy should prioritise measures that encourage domestic reform. What type of reform is seen as desirable is laid down in the Maastricht Treaty: democratisation, economic and social development, integration into the world economy (for which read, adoption of the 'free trade' religion) and a campaign against poverty.[4]

The overwhelming weight of opinion is that development policy since Maastricht has, if measured against these worthy aims, largely failed. The situation in the institutions mirrors that found so often in other areas, such as environmental or social policy. The people specifically responsible within the Commission are at least aware of the issues, even if the constraints under which they work and their own 'free market' ideologies render their efforts to address them ineffective or worse. Stray into other Directorates-General, however, and you will find the lofty goals embodied in the Commission's rhetoric readily subordinated to the supposed realities of international trade, economic growth at all costs, and the interests of the EU's multinational corporations.

11   Employment and Social Policy

Despite the fact that the European Union now takes an interest in its inhabitants as 'citizens' and not merely as workers or the people who employ them, employment and the labour market remain the priorities of EU social policy. The Social Policy Agenda adopted at the Lisbon Summit of 1999 states its objectives as 'realising Europe's full employment potential by creating more and better jobs, anticipating and managing change and adapting to the new working environment, exploiting the potential of the knowledge-based economy and promoting mobility'. In addition, however, it promises initiatives which 'centre on modernising and improving social protection', as well as 'strengthening gender equality and reinforcing fundamental rights and combating discrimination'. Not merely a labour market which functions more efficiently, creating wealth and providing widespread opportunity, but the eradication of 'poverty and exclusion and ... the integration and participation of all into [sic] economic and social life' are now the stated goals of the EU's 'social agenda', as are 'promoting gender equality' and combating discrimination in general.[1]

However, a run-through of the specific proposals annexed to this Social Agenda reveals very little in the way of concrete actions. Much talk, mountains of paper, and an extraordinary and sometimes bewildering array of jargon take the place of the kind of co-ordinated social policy of which pro-EU socialists dream and anti-EU right-wing 'sceptics' warn.[2]

The problem is not, however, simply one of rhetoric exceeding action. The creation of a single European market with no concomitant development of social protection has exerted massive downward pressure on the social and welfare systems of the member states. Cultural and language barriers, as well as the difficulties prevented by a fragmented and often bewildering housing market, have meant that far from rising, trans-frontier labour mobility rates have fallen below those of the early 1960s.[3]

From the worker's point of view, though he or she has the right to move to another member state to seek employment, in reality the situation regarding cross-border social rights and welfare benefits is confused and discouraging. Different benefits are treated differently, and the rules are so complicated that they are easily flouted by unco-operative authorities. Pressure from the Commission and Parliament has so far foundered on resistance from the member states, the richest of which have the most generous benefit systems and fear an influx of 'benefit tourists'. In addition, information about jobs in other countries can be hard to come by, especially for those with few qualifications. The EU's own employment advice and information service, Eures, is a drop in the ocean of what would be needed were a serious attempt to encourage mass labour mobility to be undertaken.[4] There are many fields, moreover, where qualifications gained in one country are not recognised in another, despite the best efforts of the European Commission over more than a decade to improve the situation.[5]

A more serious problem has been brought about by monetary union, which has deprived member states of policy alternatives which effectively cheapened labour without lowering people's incomes, if only in the short term. Devaluation of a national currency reduces the cost of a country's exports and gives govern-ments breathing space during which longer-lasting remedies to economic difficulties can be found, or the application of them given time to take effect.

A unified welfare system with high central taxation and expend-iture could compensate for this. Even in a country such as the United States, with its limited welfare and social outlays, this is a major factor in the cushioning of economic shocks. If, for example, a factory closes in Arkansas, the people who worked there stop paying income tax and some of them become eligible for welfare benefits. For these two reasons the total outflow of capital from the state is reduced. In other words, the region automatically receives a kind of aid. In addition, the state may benefit from inflows of capital in the form of federal government investment, deliberate relocation of public jobs, and so on. Former European Commission President Jacques Delors famously calculated that for the European Community to be able to create the same kind of effect it would need to have at its disposal at least 5 to 7 per cent of the total GDP of all of its member states, though even this would be considerably less than the tax take of the supposedly parsimonious US federal government. Currently, the figure is below 2 per cent and frozen at such a low rate by unanimous agreement of the EU's constituent national governments.[6]

With neither desire for nor prospect of a centralised pot of gold, and having surrendered their power to manipulate their own currencies, the EU's member states have only one means at their disposal to defend the competitiveness of their economies. They must cut labour costs. Despite much talk of efficiency savings, the only real way to achieve this is through reducing both individual wages and the 'social wage', otherwise known as the welfare state. As one right-wing economist put it: 'Behind the euro's falling exchange rate is a life-and-death struggle between it and Europe's welfare state. Either the euro subverts the welfare state, or Europe's welfare state will subvert the euro. Despite today's weakness, smart money should bet on the euro.'[7]

This puts into context the fact that the European Union has, for many years now, indulged in much hand-wringing over the persistent problem of unemployment. Whilst unemployment has numerous advantages for the 'free market' system, helping to hold down wages and generally instilling 'discipline' into the workforce, it also reduces overall purchasing power, instituting a vicious circle of low demand. In addition, it decreases state income and puts upward pressure on expenditure on welfare and social services. It adds to social division and sometimes, therefore, to strife, increasing the cost of policing. Because unemployment leads to poverty, it undermines individual health and social cohesion, with unforeseeable but undoubtedly grave consequences. In addition, of course, those touched by unemployment retain the right to vote, though a decreasing number choose to exercise it.

It was not until 1993 that the European Commission began to respond in any direct and sustained way to the phenomenon of persistent mass joblessness, or structural unemployment. Its White Paper of that year, *On Growth, Competitiveness and Employment*[8] was followed in 1994 by another on social policy.[9] Together they represented a sweeping change in rhetoric, even if real changes in substance were difficult to see, especially from the vantage point of a bench in a Job Centre in Merseyside or its equivalent in Calabria or Dresden. Since these two white papers were issued, political correctness within the EU has, as far as the subject of employment goes, revolved around what are called 'active labour market policies'. There is much talk of 'vigorous programmes of action', of 'frameworks', 'pro-active' measures and so on, as well as attempts to find a consensus by combining a dash of classical interventionism with buzzwords designed to appeal to the right, such as the specially-coined jargon words 'entrepreneurship' and 'employability'.[10]

Successive European Council summits have repeatedly drawn attention to the problem of unemployment and the urgent need to find solutions. Yet it is extremely difficult, if not impossible, to find any specific act taken by a member state which would not have been taken had the European Employment Strategy not existed. The strategy is so broad in what it allows that almost anything can be accommodated within it, at least any action likely to be taken by the great majority of member state governments, almost all of which adhere to one degree or another to neo-liberal orthodoxies.

The most enthusiastic members of the 'liberalising' school of thought, which includes Tony Blair, the Dutch Minister-President Wim Kok, and Spain's right-wing PM José María Aznar, believe that unemployment is caused almost entirely by over-regulation. For example, employers are reluctant to take on staff because it is so hard to get rid of them when they are no longer needed. Non-wage costs of employing labour, in the form, for example, of employers' contributions to social insurance or state pension schemes, are said to be too high. The ideal system is seen as that of the United States, where it is easy to hire and fire, and where the welfare state is less highly developed and therefore cheaper. The US's supposedly impressive record of job creation is held up as an example which 'Europe' should follow. Relatively high levels of unemployment are taken to mean that a country's labour market is over-regulated.

The modern US's apparent success in reducing unemployment through deregulation has been achieved by a number of methods, some of which are mere sleight of hand, whilst others would be unacceptable to almost all EU electorates – which is not quite the same, unfortunately, as saying that they will never be implemented. American workers' rights have everywhere been eroded. Wages are so low that it is now commonplace for people to have to do two or more jobs simply to survive. Many jobs carry no (or inadequate) health insurance rights, a crucial matter in a system where public health care is extremely limited. An indeterminate number of people have been bullied off the welfare rolls, to scrape a living in the informal economy, or through prostitution or crime. Over a million people, mostly young men, are in prison. America has simply replaced its unemployed by a new sub-class of working poor. It is as if we are expected to believe that the essential problem is unemployment itself, rather than the poverty it engenders. Give the poor something to do and you've solved it. Of course, this 'solution' could be imported and would undoubtedly prove the same 'success' as it has in the US.[11]

The other school of thought rejects this interpretation in favour of one which maintains a faith in the potential effectiveness of direct intervention by the state or EU authorities to promote employment. The key to a successful modern economy is seen as being a high general level of education and training. The 'flexibility' demanded of the workforce if a country's goods and services are to remain 'competitive' should be achieved by easy access to retraining and other necessary preconditions of speedy redeployment, rather than by eroding workers' rights.[12]

To some extent the UK has already adopted the American approach to unemployment, and it is hard to resist the conclusion that the Dutch government, an enthusiastically deregulating coalition, looks longingly across the Atlantic for inspiration. The strange thing is that the Netherlands, with its highly developed systems of social insurance and welfare, has unemployment at least as low as that of the US. But the Netherlands is a case in point: according to the deregulators, its success has been due to the *erosion* of regulation and social provision, not to their continuing relative strength. The same would go for Sweden, Finland and Denmark, all of which find themselves near the top of the OECD league table for recent economic performance.[13] The deregulators can never lose an argument, as their belief in neo-liberal capitalism is so fundamentalist and reductionist that everything must be twisted so that it supports their case.

Traditionally, direct EC/EU intervention in either labour market deregulation or employment creation, training and education has been limited by restraints on competence contained in the Treaty. Since the revisions of Maastricht and Amsterdam, however, competence has been extended into new areas, so that the Community can now act in the field of education as well as directly vocational training. In addition, the signing of the Charter of Fundamental Social Rights (often called the Social Charter) by all of the member states except the UK (which did not sign until after the accession of a Labour government in 1997), ushered in a new phase in which the Commission has attempted to encourage the member states to adopt what are referred to as more 'pro-active' employment policies.

The result is that the EU does now officially have an employment policy. This was initiated at the Cardiff Summit of 1997, but it was laid out in some detail at Luxembourg a year later. The refrain is a familiar one: entrepeneurship is a good thing and must not be discouraged by over-regulation and bureaucratic barriers. People, especially young people, should be given a chance to develop their skills and 'employability'. Legal frameworks, labour markets and individual enterprises should be more adaptable to the needs of a modern and changing economy. And women and men should be treated equally. Despite these agreements, member states retain competence for the development and implementation of policy. Ambiguity allows them to pursue the goals laid down at Cardiff, Luxembourg and Lisbon through directly conflicting policies.

In its report of 2000 on the implementation of the agreements made at successive summits, the European Commission was at pains to allow the member states to claim credit for the small drops in unemployment which resulted, in reality, from a mixture of economic upturn and an increased tendency in most parts of the EU to bully people into taking menial or unsuitable work. Nevertheless, it was critical of the 'uneven implementation of the four pillars' and drew attention to the need for 'increased attention to the policy mix'.[14]

It is such essentially empty phraseology which leaves the millions of the EU's unemployed, the millions more of its working poor, and those few politicians who continue to seek to represent their interests, so stubbornly unimpressed. Between 1973 and 1983, the unemployment rate for the EU15 rose from 2 per cent to 10 per cent, and it has stayed there or thereabouts ever since, peaking at 11.3 per cent in 1994. Moreover, the common-sense proposition that economic growth means more jobs has been exposed as a fallacy. Ireland, for instance, has had in recent times the highest rate of growth in the Union, averaging 4.5 per cent p.a., yet this has translated into virtual stagnation of the labour market, whose growth has been a mere 0.2 per cent a year. Of course, as always, averages mask great geographic and social disparities: areas whose wealth was based on heavy industry, mining, textiles or fishing have been particularly hard hit, as have certain groups: women, the unskilled and poorly educated, and young people have especially high rates, while a high proportion of jobless people are clearly stuck in a long-term trap: almost half of the European Union's unemployed have been without a job for over two years.[15]

HEALTH AND SAFETY AT WORK

In the same way and for the same reasons that the single market has exerted downward pressure on wages and social benefits, it has forced employers to look for ways of reducing their costs. One obvious candidate has been health and safety in the workplace. In this area, at least, the European Union has taken action.

When it comes to international measures such as the fixing of an EU-wide standard, health and safety at work is probably the least controversial area of social policy. The biggest firms with the most power and influence tend also to be the ones with the best records of health and safety, being in the main relatively heavily unionised as well as most visible to the public and enforcement authorities. For this reason, they usually find a reasonable level of health and safety protection acceptable. If common minimum standards were too lax or poorly enforced by some member-state authorities, they would lose out in competition with firms in the least vigilant countries. Nevertheless, the articles of the Treaty which give the EU competence in this area are at pains to stress that any measures must 'avoid imposing administrative, financial and legal constraints in a way which would hold back the creation and development of small and medium-sized undertakings'.[16] Though this is ostensibly designed to protect smaller firms from troublesome red tape, it can always be wheeled out as an argument against excessive (for which read effective) regulation in a particular instance where such might not suit the interests of industry.

The European Community has always enjoyed competence in this sphere and had previously conducted two 'Action Programmes', but its ability to take measures was greatly increased by the 1987 Single European Act which allowed decisions on health and safety in the workplace to be taken at Council by QMV. It was successfully argued by some governments that a unified market demanded a common minimum level of protection for workers, and the main aim was to prevent 'social dumping', where companies move to countries with lower standards in order to cut costs.

A Third Action Programme was initiated in 1987, but the most important step came in 1989 with the adoption of a 'framework directive' (i.e. one designed to make possible actions targeted at individual problems). Fourteen 'daughter' directives based on this framework (their mixed metaphor, not mine) were duly introduced, covering such matters as the safety of work equipment, personal protective equipment, working on VDUs, exposure to carcinogenic substances at work, individual industries (building, mining, quarrying, oil and gas drilling) particular groups of workers (pregnant women, young people, temporary employees) and identifiable hazards (ionising radiation, asbestos).[17]

Apart from bringing legislation up to date, the EU has, since this initial flurry of activities, also taken controversial action to limit working hours, though this emerged from its passage through the Council so full of loopholes that it is unlikely to be effective. Proposals to include certain groups of workers excluded from the initial directive (those in transport, for example) are under discussion.

A Fourth Action Programme ran from 1996 until 2000, and included the SAFE (Safety Actions for Europe) programme, through which small grants are available to small and medium-sized enterprises (SMEs) to finance practical steps to improve working conditions.[18] The EU also finances a research facility, in Bilbao, to study ways of improving workplace health and safety.[19]

This is an area of legislation which has suffered more than most from the problem of compliance and enforcement. Several member states, including the UK, have been taken to the ECJ by the Commission for failure to comply with one or another directive, either by not introducing it into national law within two years, or by weakening it during transposition.

INFORMING AND CONSULTING WORKERS

A further area in which the EU has long harboured ambitions is what it calls the 'social dialogue', the rights of workers to information, consultation and participation in the decision-making procedures which determine the policies of the enterprises in which they are employed.

An Agreement on Social Policy (ASP) appended to the Maastricht Treaty (signed by all the member states except the UK, which did not accept it until the election of a Labour government in 1997) laid down a clear system whereby, if management and unions agree, the Commission is obliged to put forward their agreement as a legislative proposal. The argument for this is that it is better for the two sides of industry, with deep knowledge of their sector, to seek a mutually acceptable solution to their problems, rather than having one imposed on them. On the other hand, the ASP removes the European Parliament from the process entirely, providing no representation for ordinary citizens whose immediate interests might also be affected. To put it simply, it is all very well for rail owners and railway workers to do deals, but what about the passengers?

This was not, of course, the British objection to it. The ASP represents a tradition of 'tri-partism', in which trade unions and employers' groups are treated almost as partners in government. It is a tradition which has deep roots in many continental countries, where Christian Democratic parties occupy more or less the same point on the political spectrum as do Britain's conservatives, and yet have their own affiliated trade unions. It is also one which had a brief heyday in 1960s and 1970s Britain, when trade unions enjoyed far more power and influence than is now the case. This was, of course, precisely what Thatcher's Tories saw as the root of all of the ills which they had been elected to cure. Having first marginalised the trade union movement and then, with the Miners' Strike of 1984–85, used every legal, extra-legal and downright illegal method she could think of to destroy it, Thatcher was not about to allow it to sneak back in from across the channel.

Though Britain has always been out on a limb, differing traditions and practices have also made it difficult for the other member states to reach agreement, and such directives which have survived their course through the Council have been extremely limited in force. The 1975 *Directive on the approximation of the laws of the Member States concerning collective redundancies*, for example, requires employers to negotiate with workers in the event of mass redundancy, a somewhat meaningless obligation and one which is, in any case, not properly enforced. This was amended in 1998, but without strengthening workers' rights. It should also be noted that a number of cases, including the notorious closure of Renault's profitable, state-of-the-art factory in Vilvoerde near Brussels in 1997, demonstrate that the Commission lacks the will to enforce even those limited rights which the Directive supposedly gives them. Other important directives are as follows:

- 1977 (amended 1998): *on the approximation of the laws of the Member States on the safeguarding of workers' rights in conjunction with the transfer of undertakings*: workers must be informed of the reasons for the transfer and the consequences.

- 1978: *on mergers of limited companies*, gives similar rights to those affected by mergers.
- 1994: *on the introduction of European Works Councils:* the first directive adopted under the ASP, it gives workers in multinational companies the right to form transnational Works' Councils which management must consult.

Proposals are also on the table to introduce worker participation on company boards or management. They are unlikely, however, to survive the attentions of the Council in anything but a severely weakened form.

EQUAL OPPORTUNITIES AND EQUAL RIGHTS FOR MEN AND WOMEN

Because of their higher unemployment rates, greater child-care responsibilities and longer life spans, women have suffered the most immediate consequences of the undermining of welfare and other social provision as a result of the Maastricht criteria for participation in EMU.[20] However, as in other areas of policy the EU has succeeded in cultivating a progressive image by means of policy initiatives which, though hugely outweighed by the damage done by other measures, are more direct and more visibly attributable to the Union.

The Treaty of Rome was certainly ahead of its day in asserting the principle that men and women should receive equal pay for equal work. It was 18 years, however, before a directive was adopted which attempted to put this into practice.[21] Further legislative measures have followed, covering access to employment, vocational training and promotion, and equality in working conditions (1976), state social security (1978), occupational social security schemes (1986 and 1996), the extending of rights to self-employed women (1986), health and safety for pregnant workers and those who have recently given birth or are breast-feeding (1992), and placing the burden of proof in cases of employment discrimination based on sex on to the employer (1996). In addition, a framework agreement on parental leave was concluded in 1996 by employers' body UNICE, the CEEP (representing smaller firms) and the European Trade Union Confederation. Two framework agreements negotiated under the ASP cover parental leave (1996) and part-time work (1997), both matters of particular interest to women.[22]

The EC/EU's competence with regard to gender discrimination did not, under the Treaty of Rome, extend beyond the workplace or matters, such as social security, closely connected with employment. Amsterdam extended it as part of a general broadening of the principle of non-discrimination to situations outside the world of work and to groups other than women.

As well as legislative measures, the EC/EU has conducted a series of Action Programmes, the fourth of which concluded in 2000. It also finances a 'Community Initiative' (Employment NOW – NOW originally took its name from 'New Opportunities for Women', an earlier Community Initiative) under the European Social Fund, specifically aimed at improving opportunities for women. The 'Employment Guidelines' around which the member states are supposed to design their annual labour market programmes specifically call for strengthened equal opportunities policies. Finally, after casting it into doubt in a case heard in 1995,[23] in 1997 the European Court of Justice upheld the legality of affirmative action in relation to areas of employment or levels of a profession where women are under-represented.[24]

DISABILITY, AGEING AND SOCIAL EXCLUSION

The EU has very limited competence in relation to issues connected with ageing, disability, and social exclusion or poverty. It has, however, undertaken a number of Action Programmes, including three aimed at disabled people (the HELIOS programmes), largely confined to sharing experiences between schemes in different member states and promoting best practice. It also supports and consults a European Disability Forum representing a range of NGOs. A Community Initiative (Horizon) provides financial support for disabled people in vocational training.[25] The 1998 and 1999 employment guidelines also draw attention to the particular difficulties facing disabled people on the labour market. Finally, following a Council Recommendation of 1997, disabled drivers can claim the same rights and privileges when visiting another member state as can residents of the country they are visiting. Proposals for improved accessibility to public transport vehicles have so far foundered in Council, largely due to the expense.

The 'mainstreaming' of disability policy called for in a 1996 Commission Communication has made little progress. New anti-

discrimination provisions introduced at Amsterdam have given the
EU more potential to act, but the results are still awaited.

The EU has even less competence to act in relation to retired
people than it does over disability. Pensions remain the exclusive
province of the member states, as does the power to establish a
minimum income, housing conditions, and health care. Taken
together, this means that the major determinants of quality of life for
people beyond the age of retirement are dealt with by national and
local authorities.

This has not prevented the Commission from instigating an
Action Programme (1991–93), and a European Year of the Elderly
and Solidarity between the Generations (1993). This attempt to reach
out of its area of competence was curtailed in 1996 when the UK
Conservative government successfully contested the Commission's
plans to allocate ECU 6.5m of the 1996 budget for measures on
behalf of the elderly.

A similar fate met the Commission's attempts to address poverty.
These have always been limited, and the EC/EU has little
competence in relevant areas. Nevertheless, three small 'poverty
programmes' consisting of supposedly innovative 'pilot programmes', locally-based schemes to alleviate some of the
consequences of poverty for the most part, were financed, as were a
number of international conferences. The fourth programme,
however, which should have run from mid-1994 to 1999, was
abandoned following a challenge from the UK and later Germany.

EDUCATION AND TRAINING

Prior to Maastricht, an artificial division had arisen within EC policy-
making, between 'training' on the one hand and 'education' on the
other. The reasons for the division were understandable. The
Community began life ostensibly as a purely economic project:
'training' implies preparation for a job, in other words to take one's
place as a productive member of the economy. 'Education', on the
other hand, has (or ought to have) a major non-vocational element.
Given that a large part of this, at least in most countries, has to do
with national culture, tradition and religious and other beliefs, the
member states were wary of handing over competence to a supra-
national body. In practice, by the 1980s education aimed at adults
(including university-level courses) was seen as a legitimate area of

interest for the Community. This was formalised at Maastricht and Amsterdam, so that now the EU has limited but clear competence over education as well as training.

The aims of the EU's contribution to education are propagandistic ('to make citizens of the Community more aware of the role which the latter plays in their everyday lives ... (and) add a European dimension to the education and training of pupils and teachers'), moral ('to ... foster mutual understanding between peoples'), and practical ('to ... enable the Community to be actively involved in all areas of research, technology and higher education'). This last might also be seen as propagandistic, of course, but its practical purpose is to feed into the limited co-ordination of research and development which is also an EU priority. Since the development of an EU employment policy, moreover, training programmes are expected to serve the aims of that policy, with 'employability' given prominence amongst the inevitable jargon.

Available funds are small and in the past have been concentrated on the Comett, Erasmus and Lingua programmes, the latter two of which have now been superseded by a single programme, Socrates, supplemented by a training programme, Leonardo. Comett began life in 1987 as a programme to finance transnational training projects involving new technologies. Projects involve co-operation between universities and the private sector enterprises. Erasmus helped pay for student exchanges between universities in different member states. Lingua, as the name suggests, was concerned with improving language skills by giving support to member states' initiatives in the field.

Socrates continues the higher education elements of the earlier programmes, but also includes initiatives lower down the age scale, whilst Leonardo is an attempt to rationalise the older COMETT programme and a number of small sectoral training initiatives.[26]

THE EUROPEAN SOCIAL FUND

A much more significant source of support for vocational training is the European Social Fund (ESF), the main financial tool through which the European Union translates its strategic employment policy aims into action. With the exception of a very small amount disbursed under what are known as the Community Programmes (CPs), it is the authorities of the member states which decide who gets this money, although this is done within the context of the employment guidelines approved by the Commission and Council. The ESF usually provides 'matching' funding for training and other employment initiatives, though this is usually in the form of 'matching funds': an equal, or some, proportion of the money needed for a project must come from national sources. ESF funds concentrate on poorer regions and those with problems brought about by economic change – for example, those areas historically dependent on heavy industries. The idea is to generate a virtuous circle through which private capital will be attracted to these regions. In addition, the ESF attempts to encourage international co-operation, the sharing of best practices, and innovative approaches to the problems involved.

Following the reform of the Structural Funds at the beginning of 2000, the ESF was given five priorities:

- Development of active labour market policies to combat and prevent unemployment, to avoid long-term unemployment, to facilitate the reintegration of the long-term unemployed and to support integration into the labour market of young people and persons returning to work after a period of absence.
- Promotion of equal opportunities for all in terms of access to the labour market, with particular attention to persons at risk of social exclusion.
- Promotion and improvement of vocational training, education and counselling in the context of a lifelong learning policy.
- Promotion of a skilled, well-trained and flexible workforce, innovative and adaptable forms of work organisation, and entrepreneurship.
- Specific measures to improve access and active participation of women in the labour market (career prospects, access to new job opportunities, setting up businesses, etc.).[27]

12 The Environment

It was not until 1973 that the European Community established its modest first Environmental Action Programme; yet, by the end of the century environmental law had become a major feature of European Union activity. This was in part, of course, simply because of the increasing urgency and seriousness of such problems as pollution of seas, waterways and the atmosphere, climate change, contaminated food and new technologies. It also, insofar as it was made possible only by extending Community competence, reflects a long-term weakening of resistance to integrationism.

Whatever their views about this European Union, few people doubt that, because almost all environmental problems have a trans-frontier dimension, international decision-making bodies are needed to confront them. In practice, however, the member states, whilst recognising this, have been reluctant to hand over the sort of power which might, in theory, enable the EU's centralised institutions to get to grips with the environment. Given that EC/EU policies have done a great deal to bring about the environmental crisis which we are facing, member states can hardly be blamed for hesitating before handing over powers to tax, fine and subsidise – the 'instruments' which the European Commission has proposed to the Council, on a number of occasions, as a means to further environmental policy. The Common Agricultural Policy, which gives the European Union more centralised power than it enjoys in any other area, is hardly inspiring as a green credential.

Whilst specific pieces of legislation have often met with a degree of success, this has been offset by a clear failure to adopt a coherent overall strategy and the virtual collapse of attempts to green other areas of policy such as those affecting industry and transport, as well as the notorious CAP itself. Much-vaunted agricultural reform has led to a widespread assumption that the structural problems afflicting EU agriculture have somehow been dealt with, or at least that things are better than they were. In fact, the impact of the inadequate steps taken has so far been extremely limited, doing little to halt the ravaging of the countryside.

The arrival of genetically modified crops, set to take off following the reform in 2001 of the system governing their approval, shows that the caution induced by the BSE and dioxin scandals melts away all too quickly in the heat of market imperatives. In addition to the damage wrought by the CAP, the EU must answer for the billions of euros of structural fund money spent on worthless or damaging projects for roads, dams, airports and all the rest of an unlovely and poorly-planned infrastructure. Afforestation programmes destroy traditional landscapes and replace them with serried ranks of alien species of trees, woods which undermine bio-diversity and can cause untold and unpredictable damage to water courses and other features of environmental, economic and aesthetic importance. And all of this is carried out despite the ostensible requirement for an Environmental Impact Assessment (EIA) for most major infrastructure projects.[1]

Subsidies are paid for unmarketable crops – Greek tobacco, most notoriously, but also the environmentally destructive rice plantations of Northern Italy – and then further subsidies given to enable their export. Meanwhile, the CAP's troublesome little brother, the Common Fisheries Policy, has failed to save either the fish or those who catch them from near and possibly imminent extinction.

The drive for a single internal market at all costs has also produced anomalies which can range from the absurd to the catastrophic. Potatoes, grown in Northern Germany, are driven south to be washed and packed, then taken back to their birthplace for sale. Apples are driven back and forth, traded between member states, despite the fact that almost every EU country grows them. If this meant greater variety, at least there would be some point to it; in fact, the range and variety of apples available in each member state has declined as a direct result of the CAP, as well as of the intensified competition brought about by the single market. The necessary transport requires infrastructure, of course, which generally means roads. These are built, moreover, at the taxpayers' expense, despite the fact that the vast majority gain nothing whatsoever from the deal.

The term 'mainstreaming' was probably first used in relation to equal opportunities policy. It indicates that a particular goal (gender equality, a healthy environment) is borne in mind whenever policy is formulated, not merely when policy is formulated which from the outset is aimed at that goal. For example, the point of building a road is not to improve the environment but to make it easier for people and goods to get to and from the places served by the road; but a 'mainstreamed' environment policy would set out to ensure that the road was absolutely necessary, that it was built with as little damage as possible, and that it met criteria based on an ecologically conscious cost-benefit analysis. Mainstreaming has been incorporated into the Treaty since Amsterdam, whose Article 3D states that 'environmental protection requirements must be integrated into the definition and implementation of Community policies and activities ...' These fine words, however, remain a long way from being translated into any discernible impact.[2]

PROGRAMMES, POLICIES, PROBLEMS

The EU understandably likes to play down such concerns in favour of concentrating on its specific achievements in combating pollution and other scourges. Even here, however, many such 'achievements' fail to stand up to a little close scrutiny. Even where it has not been an abject failure, most EU legislation has fallen well short of the original goals.

To pursue its aims, the EU is able to use powers granted under the Single European Act (SEA) of 1987, which specifically assigned the Community competence over environmental policy. Since further reforms at Maastricht and Amsterdam, environmental policy is subject in general to the co-decision procedure and to Qualified Majority Voting at Council. This gives the European Parliament a relatively powerful role, and its Committee on the Environment, Public Health and Consumer Affairs deals with more legislative matters than does any other EP committee. In addition, Amsterdam added 'sustainable development' to the fundamental objectives of the Union listed in Article 2 of the Treaty, building on Maastricht's alteration of the 'economic growth' of the Treaty of Rome to 'sustainable and non-inflationary growth which respects the environment'.[3]

The EU organises itself around what are known as Environmental Action Programmes (EAPs). The first four EAPs ran from 1973 to 1992 and resulted in the adoption of around 200 pieces of legislation. The bulk of these introduced minimum standards to limit pollution and govern the disposal of waste. The Fifth Environmental Action Programme ends in 2000 and plans for a Sixth are under discussion.[4] The Fifth EAP – *Towards sustainability* – was also the first to give prominence to the idea of a 'horizontal approach' which would affect policies whose primary purpose was not environmental. Industrial policy, energy, transport, and individual sectors such as agriculture, fisheries and tourism would henceforth be expected to take account of the principles of sustainable development. Of course, in practice huge pressures work in a direction antagonistic to such a principle: the enormous influence of big corporations on EU decision-making, the environmentally destructive methods imposed by the CAP, the obligations entered into by the Union and its members in the World Trade Organisation (WTO) and other international agreements.

Proposals affecting the interests of a particular industry are met with enormous organised resistance from armies of professional lobbyists whose resources environmentalist organisations cannot hope to match. Legislation tends to be most successful when it accords with the interests of industry, especially if that industry is dominated by big corporations and located predominantly in one of the powerful member states. Thus, whilst the idea that German corporations care one way or the other about the environment is faintly absurd, the fact that they care about their competitiveness is self-evident. Relatively strong regulation in a powerful member state can thus mean that, in some cases, its government and industry leaders actually demand stronger measures elsewhere. The cut-and-thrust of member states' manoeuvring in the Council does allow, also, for a certain amount of horse trading or, to give it its polite European name, 'package dealing'. Poorer states can sometimes be persuaded to accept higher standards by offers of financial assistance, or trades can be made along the lines of 'you vote for my tight emission controls and I'll make sure you don't have to do anything about enabling disabled people to use your public transport'. The results are, to put it kindly, patchy, as one would expect from a body of legislation driven by commercial considerations rather than genuine concern for the long-term future of the planet or the immediate wellbeing of the people who live on it.

Not all EU environmental measures, however, are taken wholly or even partly in the name of the single market. Pressure also comes from public opinion, of course, and no doubt even from the critical nature of what is happening to the planet. Restrictions which do not overly inconvenience corporate industry or agriculture have always a chance of seeing the statute books. It is, however, highly significant that the first environmental proposals to be dealt with by QMV – following the Single European Act of 1987 – were those which affected the internal market. Whilst this was a clever way to get a foot in the door, the priorities it takes for granted are disturbing. To trade is, apparently, more important than to breathe clean air or drink fresh water. Maastricht extended QMV to almost all aspects of environmental policy, but these priorities have not changed at all.

The usefulness of policies emerging from these conflicting pressures varies hugely. Widespread criticism of the Fifth EAP illustrates this. Its effectiveness was widely seen as undermined by vague and sometimes unrealistic targets, and avoidance wherever possible of binding measures. Following the principle of subsidiarity, member states were given major responsibility for implementing the programme, but this created a problem of monitoring and enforcement which they seemed ill-inclined to address. It is hard to escape the conclusion that member-state governments are happy enough to purchase a green image with their successors' money, agreeing to expensive measures knowing that, whilst they will get the credit, they will be retired or out of office before the bill arrives.

Enforcement has never been Brussels' strength. In the 1980s, the Third Action Programme devoted all of three lines to the problem of implementation. Even now, the Directorate General for Environment lacks the enforcement powers and personnel enjoyed by those which deal, for example, with competition policy or fisheries. Implementation is also not aided by the fact that individuals have no right to proceed against their governments for non-compliance with EU law, a right which exists, for example, in the realm of employment-related legislation.

The Fifth Programme was particularly ineffective in relation to agriculture. This reflects a broader problem, that the methods encouraged by the CAP are so environmentally corrosive that attempting to ameliorate their damage without abolishing the system completely is futile. The CAP turns any attempt to provide incentives to support good environmental practices into no more than a sop, a drop in the ocean of pollution and devastation for which it is responsible.

The EU is also criticised for having failed to pursue its goals in ways which would be likely to bring about the co-operation or compliance of those whose behaviour would have to change if these goals were to be achieved: corporations, governments and individual consumers. The member states' wariness in the face of any attempt to extend Community competence into the realm of taxation has so far prevented acceptance of EU financial instruments which might help to achieve this. Contained within the Fifth EAP were ambitious plans for a combined energy/CO_2 tax, a tax on nitrogen and agricultural pesticides. The European Parliament has, in addition, called for taxes on water, waste, and tourism, but these too have fallen foul of member-state hostility.[5]

Whether the Sixth Environmental Action Programme will succeed in remedying these defects remains to be seen.[6] Proposed priorities include climate change, the environment and health, protecting nature and biodiversity, and resource and waste management. These are so broad as to be almost meaningless, of course. If the EU is to build on its limited and partial successes in reducing industrial emissions of harmful gases and particles, cuts in phosphorus, lead and mercury in the general environment, or reduced acidification of forests and water courses, then it will need to use these broad categories as a starting point for tough, specific and well-targeted action. Its past record does not bode well.

PUBLIC HEALTH

Public health policy is often classed with environmental matters. The European Parliament Committee on Environment, for example, also deals with public health. However, its history as a subject of EU competence is much more recent. Not until Maastricht did policy in this area acquire a legal base. On this basis, eight Public Health Programmes have since been established, dealing with health promotion, monitoring, AIDS and other communicable diseases, cancer, rare diseases, injury prevention, and pollution-related diseases.

In addition, reports have been produced on, *inter alia,* the safety of human blood and blood products, the integration of health concerns into other EU policies, and tobacco, and a network established on the surveillance and control of communicable diseases. EU competence remains extremely limited and its actions are confined to supporting programmes and actions initiated by the member states and ensuring the dissemination of the results of such actions in order to encourage the spread of 'best practices'.[7]

13 The Common Agricultural Policy and Common Fisheries Policy

The Common Agricultural Policy, the most important and costly of European Community actions, was constructed in the 1950s by people whose memories of depression and war were still fresh. It was designed to ensure that the people of the six founder states would never again go hungry. In meeting this aim it has been spectacularly successful, delivering a quantity and variety of food which has ensured that all but the very poorest have access to an adequate diet. Why, then, is the CAP, more than any other aspect of the European integrationist project, not only the *bête noire* of sceptics and opponents of the Union, but an embarrassment to its staunchest supporters?

The CAP's central goal is to increase agricultural productivity whilst guaranteeing the incomes of farmers, stabilising markets and assuring the food supply. Although one of its stated aims is to ensure reasonable prices for the consumer, it has always worked by raising the price of food above that which prevails on the world market.

Article 39 of the Treaty of Rome promises a policy which offers farmers a reasonable standard of living on the basis of stable market conditions and, for consumers, affordable prices and security of supply. Article 40 then offers a choice of ways in which these goals might be achieved. There was to be, however, in every case, a common Community organisation of markets. Only the means to achieve this differed.

What makes agriculture a special phenomenon within the EU is Article 42, which states that specific provisions of the CAP take precedence over normal competition rules.[1] It seems that free markets, whose wonders are reckoned limitless when it comes to the distribution of the baubles of twenty-first-century consumerism, are not to be trusted with the prosaic business of filling our bellies or, indeed, farmers' pockets. Although modification of this original blanket exemption began almost immediately, in many striking ways the CAP continues to remove agriculture from the hurly-burly of increasingly liberalised capitalism, though state aids are subject to the same rules as apply in other sectors.

How then, does the CAP work? Firstly, on the basis of Common Market Organisations (CMOs), which remove obstacles to trade in primary agricultural products between member states, a number of aims are pursued: farmers' incomes are enhanced by pricing regimes which maintain prices at an artificially high level, one which is above world prices. In addition to the principle of an internal, barrier-free market, the CAP is based on Community Preference, the use, in other words, of protectionist devices to prevent imported products from being sold at lower prices than are their EU-grown equivalents, a policy which has become increasingly controversial as 'free trade' has driven all other notions of how international commerce might be managed into the margins of political and economic thought. Bucking this trend, the EU fixes a threshold price, a minimum under which products may not be imported. Finally, the CAP is supposed to perform a redistributive function: the European Agricultural Guidance and Guarantee Fund (EAGGF) is designed to redress any economic disruption brought about by decisions taken under the CAP.

Specifically, financial assistance may be granted to help lagging regions to catch up; to contribute to the development of rural regions in difficult circumstances which are not poor enough to benefit as ERDF Objective 1 areas; to speed up adjustment of agricultural structures where this is made necessary by changing market conditions; to maintain viable communities in less-favoured regions; to aid the establishment of young farmers; and to enhance efficiency, promote diversification or improve marketing or processing, for example by encouraging the setting-up of producers' associations.

Prices of agricultural commodities are set each year by the Council. In fixing these prices, the Council takes account of overall inflation, as well as market conditions such as good and poor harvests or unusual rises or falls in demand. This price is, however, merely a target, and market conditions may put it under pressure. If the actual price farmers are receiving falls too far below the guide price, to a level known as the 'intervention price' (or 'basic price' in the case of meat from pigs), then an intervention organisation in each member state is legally obliged to buy and store the product in question. Where food which is too perishable to be stored is concerned (mainly fruit and vegetables), the relevant level is known as the withdrawal price. In such cases surplus produce is, where possible, distilled into industrial alcohol, given to voluntary sector groups who organise its distribution to those in need, or, if all else fails, destroyed. It is this aspect of the CAP which tends to lead to vividly bad publicity, with pictures of tomatoes being ploughed into the sea appearing on the TV news, tales of insurmountable butter mountains and wine lakes of Atlantic dimensions, or widespread resentment brought about by what always seem to be ill-advised and poorly-organised food distribution schemes. Destruction may also be avoided by exporting surplus produce. Export subsidies are paid to make this worthwhile, but the damaging consequences, particularly for farmers in poor countries driven off the land by the availability of low-priced imports, as well as the general distortion of competition such subsidies bring about, has led to the EU's agreeing to restrict this system to a specified list of commodities and to a smaller overall volume. Bilaterally agreed tariff reductions under what is known as the Generalised System of Preferences (GSP), and EU obligations negotiated under the Lomé Convention, in the framework of the United Nations Conference on Trade and Development, and with the applicant countries of central and eastern Europe and the Mediterranean, have also greatly reduced the scope of export subsidies.

Criticism of the CAP has long been severe, and it has focused on more than one aspect of the system. Firstly, there is the sheer expense. Although in proportional terms spending has declined since the early 1990s, this disguises an absolute increase of around 50 per cent over the decade. The latest reform, moreover, agreed at the Berlin Summit of March, 1999, will see spending rise still further in the period 2000–06. Overall, the CAP now accounts for just under half of the EU's annual expenditure.

If this resulted in lower food prices it might constitute an effective redistributive mechanism, as the poorer an individual or family, the greater proportion of net income is spent on food. Unfortunately, however, precisely the opposite is the case, as the CAP inflicts a double burden of artificially high prices, coupled with taxation, to maintain prices paid to farmers at around double the level found on the world market. According to the British government, the Common Agricultural Policy cost consumers in the UK £6.7b in 1998, on top of a tax bill of £3.4b, equivalent to £3.30 per person per week.[2]

Criticism has also come from trading partners who object to the exclusion of agriculture from what are now, under the WTO, the normal rules of world trade, where subsidies and artificial encouragement to domestic industries are severely restricted. Finally, even the supposed beneficiary of all this, the farmer, is suffering. Despite being virtually forced by the rules of the CAP to employ the most environmentally destructive methods, farmers in most member states have seen their incomes decline. The smaller the farm, the more likely this is to be the case, with the result that the devastation of nature is compounded by the wholesale destruction of rural communities.[3]

As well as failing to give them effective support, moreover, the CAP traps farmers into a bewildering maze of bureaucracy. Not only does this waste time which might be better employed farming, but the CAP's bizarre procedures also offer huge opportunities for fraud, which has been estimated to drain at least 10 per cent from its budget. Since the late 1980s, attempts have been made at reforms which would fulfil the EU's obligations under the GATT to reduce and eventually eliminate subsidies, whilst avoiding the building up of food mountains and preserving the countryside, its population and environment. These attempts have, however, foundered on the rocks of farming interests. The latest, urgently necessitated by the prospect of enlargement, was unable to make headway for the usual reasons: the interests of different groups of farmers, and therefore of different member states, are in irreconcilable conflict.

THE COMMON FISHERIES POLICY

European fisheries are, like those in most of the rest of the world, in crisis. All the signs indicate that, unless drastic action is taken, humanity is in danger of exhausting what has been one of its major sources of food for possibly tens of thousands of years. The equation does not work out. Too much of the fish stock has been pulled from the ocean for purposes which are wasteful and following policies which are short-sighted in the extreme. The Common Fisheries Policy has manifestly failed to tackle this problem. It has allowed factory ships to plunder waters traditionally fished by relatively sustainable methods, waters upon which whole communities depended for their livelihoods. It has produced unfair catch divisions between national fleets, causing persistent antagonisms between member states. It has failed to protect either the fish, the men and women who make their livings from them, or the consumer. Of all the EU's policies, it is the most spectacular and persistent failure.

In 1999 the EU fleet totalled around 97,000 vessels (down from almost 100,000 in 1996) producing over 8m tonnes of fish. The Union is also a net importer of fish. Fleet capacity has declined in recent years, with the EU contributing through its structural funds to the decommissioning of old vessels and the modernisation of fleets.[4] Vigorous efforts have been made to reform the CFP and make it into an effective instrument for conservation. Fish conservation cannot possibly be effective without input from other policy areas. Sustainable fishing depends first of all on a healthy marine environment, requiring reforms of industrial methods, waste disposal, transport policies and so on. It is much more than a matter of how much fish you take. Other important factors are the mix of species caught, the size and age of the fish, the point in their reproductive cycle at which they are killed, the techniques used in catching them and the waters from which they are taken. All of this requires agreement, regulation, and, most difficult to achieve, effective enforcement.[5]

In addition, a successful fisheries policy would involve employment and social measures to enhance or replace fishing as a source of livelihood for those dependent on the industry. Fishing towns are characteristically remote and few offer ready sources of alternative employment. Although the fishing sector's contribution to GNP is generally less than 1 per cent, its impact is disproportionate in those areas where it is a major source of employment. Closures of fishing grounds or slumps in the industry can therefore have particularly devastating consequences. Overall, only around a quarter of a million people, almost all of them men, are directly employed in the catching of fish. However, behind this stands an army of workers in processing, packing, transport and marketing, as well as those who produce fishing gear, vessels and other necessities of the industry.

First adopted in its current form in 1983, the CFP has four main elements: a policy for conservation, including enforcement of rules; a structural policy, designed to enable the industry to adapt to changes in supply and demand; a marketing policy; and finally a policy governing relations with Third Countries. Fish stocks need to be renewed, of course, and to this end young fish need to be left to mature and reproduce. The CFP attempts to set maximum quantities of fish that can safely be caught every year. Known as Total Allowable Catches (TACs), these are divided among member states as 'national quota'. To limit the capture of small fish, minimum mesh sizes may be fixed, known breeding or maturation areas closed to fishing, and certain types of gear banned. Of course, each of these methods generates controversy whenever the CFP is renegotiated.

Overall, the EU has tried to reduce the size of the total fleet and modernise what remains, making grants available for both purposes. For each member state with a fishing industry, fleet restructuring is planned according to multi-annual guidance programmes setting out objectives and the means to achieve them.

The nature of fishing also makes it necessary to develop agreements with Third Countries. Since the establishment of the EEC, and at the initiative of heavily fishing-dependent nations such as Iceland, the extent of the coastal exclusion zone from which a country may legally exclude foreign boats has increased hugely, necessitating a series of new agreements. The EU has also negotiated access to the waters of poor neighbouring states by offering compensation in other areas of trade or development policy.

The CFP works through a series of national Multi-annual Guidance Programmes for the fishing fleets (MAGPs), plans which are devised by each member state with an industry and then approved by Commission and Council. A new MAGP is set to start at the beginning of 2002 and will have to take into account the very large cuts in quotas agreed by the member states. The MAGPs must be designed according to rules laid down in a Regulation which contains specific provisions on fleet renewal and the modernisation of fishing vessels, the adjustment of fishing effort, the creation of joint enterprises, public aid for fleet renewal and vessel modernisation, small-scale coastal fishing, socio-economic measures, the development of aquatic resources, aquaculture, fishing-port facilities, processing, marketing and promotion, measures to find new market outlets, producer organisations, compensation to fishermen and vessel owners for temporary cessation of activities, inland fishing, support for pilot projects and technical assistance.

In December 2000 the fisheries ministers of the member states finally faced up to the reality of the fact that the fish were disappearing. Announcing devastating cuts in TACs, as well as a total suspension of cod fishing, they forced the fishing communities of the member states, as well as EU consumers, to pay the price of four decades of mismanagement. At the dawn of the twenty-first century, what had until relatively recently been a major source of protein for many of the continent's poorest people was in danger of becoming a luxury that only the very rich could afford.

14   Transport

It has always been the intention of the European Community to develop a Common Transport Policy (CTP) and, on paper, the CTP came into being with the Treaty of Rome. The initial problem was to cure the member states of the border habit, making it as easy to travel and shift goods between them as it was within the frontiers of a single state. Until the mid-1980s, however, these attempts proved a miserable failure, making something of a mockery of the idea that the Community indeed had a unified transport policy, or even that it was a genuine 'Common Market' at all. A second aim of the CTP, the right of carriers from one member state to offer services in another, seemed even further from realisation.

One of the major priorities of the drive to create a single EU internal market was to overcome the continuing national control of transport systems, enforce liberalisation and bring about, on this basis, a more unified system. Much of this has been achieved, which may be why transport has become cheaper whilst steadily decreasing in reliability and contributing an ever-greater share of air pollution, climate change, noise and a host of other forms of social damage. In road transport, at least, national markets have largely been opened, and carriers from one member state are free to offer services in another, even – and this was for many years the great sticking point – where both the place of departure and the destination were in the same country.

In addition to problems specific to transport, the attempt to revive the CTP faced all the usual difficulties of the single market project: incompatible national standards regarding technical specifications; rules governing workforce conditions, safety and the environment which differed greatly in stringency; difficulties (particularly acute in the case of transport, which was characterised by a high proportion of public ownership) in enforcing rules on state aids and other aspects of competition policy and the fact that not everyone was (or is) convinced that liberalisation was a good thing. Efforts have been more successful in some sectors than others, and in transport there remains a great deal to be done before we arrive at the free market EUtopia dreamed of by the Union's ideologues.

Despite ongoing problems in the transport sector, in general the internal market project launched by the Single European Act was, in its own terms, a remarkable success. Increased intra-Community trade was one of the phenomena which fuelled rapid growth in transport, with cross-border traffic increasing by 2.4 per cent per year between 1980 and 1994, and such growth has shown no signs of abating. Figures for the most environmentally damaging, dangerous and socially destructive forms of transport, moreover, are even more impressive. In the same 15-year period road freight increased by 3.5 per cent per annum, whilst air passenger traffic grew by a massive 7.8 per cent during the 1980s, dropping to 6.1 per cent at the end of the decade. Freight movements by rail, on the other hand, actually declined slightly during the 1980s and more steeply in the 1990s. Water traffic, both inland and sea, did increase, but by a rate so low that the Commission has described its performance as 'stagnant'.[1] The Commission argues that overall levels of transport cannot be reduced, surely a controversial assertion but one for which it produces neither evidence nor arguments, accepting it as given. Instead, it has proposed, originally in a 1992 White Paper, a new approach based on the following principles:

- 'Intermodality': transport will be treated as a single system, capable of coherence and co-ordination.
- 'Trans-European Networks (TENs)': closing gaps, so that all parts of the Union can be interconnected.
- Fair pricing, with 'external costs' such as environmental damage, factored in.
- Protecting the environment.
- Safety.
- Good working conditions.
- Strengthening the internal market.

The White Paper identified the central problem as rapidly approaching saturation, with road traffic, which accounts for the bulk of growth, being in greatest danger of grinding to a halt, especially in certain regions and routes which were identified as 'congestion "black spots"'. Despite growth, moreover, spending on transport infrastructure was falling in relation to Gross National Product. Transport growth, concentrated on roads, was responsible for an increasing amount of atmospheric pollution and noise, despite improvements in vehicle emissions and the advent of quieter vehicles. Technological progress which should have led to cleaner air and quieter streets was being undermined by the rocketing numbers of cars and lorries on the roads. To tackle these problems the Commission instituted an Action Programme, designed to run from 1995 to 2000. A new Action Programme, 'Sustainable Mobility', overlapped with it, however, running from 1998 to 2004.[2]

The Action Programme is based partly on the principle, laid out in a Green Paper of 1995 and the subsequent White Paper, *Fair payment for infrastructure use: a phased approach to a common transport infrastructure charging framework in the EU* (1998). At the same time, a new White Paper detailed plans to restructure the system. It was supplemented in 1998 by a report from the Commission setting out ways in which the environmental problems, especially those related to CO_2 emissions, could be addressed.[3] They include technological improvements which, as they are in any case in the interests of the powerful motor and road haulage industries (you don't have to be an eco-warrior to want to use less fuel), will probably see the light of day. More problematic are the goals of transferring more freight back to rail, encouraging the use of public transport, and making transport users cover the real costs of their chosen mode (ending, in other words, the hidden subsidisation of private transport by 'internalising external costs' – an incorporation of the 'polluter pays' principle).

The car industry and road haulage lobbies are simply so powerful that it is virtually impossible to put through legislative measures which are inimical to their interests, and none of these problems can be alleviated without such measures. This largely explains the gap between Commission rhetoric and the toothless measures which emerge at the other end of the process.

This is symptomatic of two broader problems within transport policy, one which troubles integrationists and another which should trouble everyone. The first is that the Commission's claim that the EU now has a Common Transport Policy is, to put it kindly, over-optimistic. The Commission itself complains, for example, that each member state uses quite different methods to finance its system: different levels of tax and subsidy with little attempt to make these fair or coherent in relation to the real costs of each mode, different ways of collecting revenues, and so on.[4] Member states continue to run more-or-less independent national transport policies, though in the last few years these have come under heavy pressure from the liberalisation frenzy which has gripped the Commission.

Even the lesser objective of a CTP which controls international, intra-EU traffic is far from being fulfilled. As one pro-EU writer has put it, what we have now is not a 'common policy for the transport sector ... replacing the essential elements of national policies', but rather 'a Community policy ... which only coordinates and supplements national policies.'[5]

The second problem is the gap between the Commission's environmentally-friendly words and the actual behaviour of the European Union. To accept that transport volumes will continue to increase, as the Commission says it does, may be reprehensible or realistic, depending on one's viewpoint. To pretend that it is an inexorable phenomenon entirely outside the control of political authorities is, however, simply dishonest. In fact, it is the EU's policy of subordinating everything to the completion of a single internal market which has made a major contribution to this increase, a fact of which the Commission is usually quite proud. To serve the resultant increase in the long- and medium-distance movement of goods the EU has created the legal conditions for, and helped to finance, massive construction of new transport infrastructure. A Swiss attempt – approved by referenda in 1994 and 1998 – to impose swingeing levies on road goods vehicles crossing their country and to ban them completely from 2004 was met by a threat from the Union of extensive economic sanctions, with a consequent softening of the Swiss approach.[6] The Commission now predicts that freight transport across the Alps will increase by 75 per cent between 1992 and 2010, no doubt due to inexorable, impersonal forces.[7]

Instead of tackling the urgently needed task of reducing road traffic, the Commission prefers to 'work with the industry' (generally a euphemism for producing weak proposals which please corporate lobbyists) to cut pollution from each individual vehicle. The Auto-Oil Programme, for example, will institute mandatory standards governing exhaust emissions, to be brought into force in 2005. An originally weak Commission proposal was rejected by both Council and Parliament, resulting in a massive lobbying effort by the industry. In the end, the Council and Parliament agreed a compromise which, if the projected doubling of road traffic in the next decade occurs, will not result in cleaner air or a slowing down of climate change. At least the Auto-Oil Programme is a legislative measure. It does not, however, cover emissions of the major greenhouse gas, carbon dioxide (CO_2). These are governed only by a voluntary agreement with manufacturers, in return for which the EU has promised not to introduce compulsory standards until 2008.

The details of other policies are no more encouraging. The solution to rail's problems is believed to be deregulation and liberalisation, though evidence for this bizarre view is hard to come by, especially in the United Kingdom, where it led to the virtual collapse of the system. Fortunately, many member-state governments are unconvinced.

TRANS EUROPEAN TRANSPORT NETWORKS (TENS)

The Treaty on European Union, which came into force in November 1993, established Trans-European networks in transport, energy and telecommunications. They were designed to address the problem that the development of the internal market has, so it is argued, been hampered by the reality that transport systems, like energy and telecommunications infrastructures, were designed to serve separate countries rather than to facilitate travel between them.

TENs are financed by a mix of EU, member-state and private finance and will cost an estimated 400b euros by 2010. The Commission's proposal is for 70,000 km of railways, including 22,000 km of new and upgraded track for High Speed Trains, 15,000 km of new roads, combined transport corridors and terminals, 267 airports, and networks of inland waterways and sea ports.

The Commission claims that TENs will help fuel growth, and that this will bring jobs, benefiting everyone; that peripheral regions will benefit from improved links; that applicant countries' integration will be facilitated and other neighbours will benefit from improved links with the wealthy EU; it even states they will reduce traffic congestion and, consequently, pollution. TENs, says the Commission, 'embody the concept of sustainable mobility which seeks to improve the environment and preserve tomorrow's natural resources without sacrificing today's economic growth'.

Not everyone is convinced, however. Critics argue that TENs are too expensive, that too much is being spent on roads, that most of the investment in rail is in High Speed Trains which offer few benefits to ordinary people and are less environmentally advantageous than a major investment in short- and medium-distance conventional rail. In addition, little has been done to produce reasoned proof of the economic benefits of TENs. At this stage of research, the claim that TENs will enhance regional economies is no more plausible than the counter-claim that they will lead to more centralisation of production in already prosperous areas.[8]

Box 14.1

The Problems

In the European Union:
Transport services are provided to a total value of over 500b euros (€) a year. The transport sector thus accounts for 4% of the European Union's GDP.

During the 1980s and 1990s, the transport sector grew 2.3% a year for freight and 3.1% for passengers over the last 20 years.

6m people, or 4.2% of the total working population, are employed in transport. This number increases to 14m if we add those employed in the transport equipment industry and all those working in transport-related businesses.

€ 70b are invested each year in transport infrastructure, equivalent to 1% of the EU's GDP.

Household spending each year on transport totals € 600b. On average this is 14% of each household's annual income.

Each individual travels an average of 35 km each day using one means of transport or another.

Road freight transport more than doubled between 1970 and 1995.

42, 000 people die on the roads every year.

Transport is responsible for 26% of CO_2 emissions. On current trends this will rise to 40% by 2010. Road transport is the biggest source of CO_2 and urban traffic generates half of all CO_2 emissions. Private cars are responsible for some 50% of road transport emissions and road haulage for about 35%. Between 1985 and 1995 there was a rise of nearly 36% in the level of CO_2 emissions generated by road transport. Air traffic produces 12% of transport-related CO_2 emissions, but the level is rising by 6% a year. Transport by rail, inland waterway and sea is less energy-intensive. As a result of the switch to road, the level of CO_2 emissions from transport is rising faster then economic growth. This is partly due to the rise in the proportion of road transport.

Source: European Commission Directorate General for Transport and Energy, *Towards Sustainable Mobility* at http://europa.eu.int/comm/transport/themes/mobility/english/sm_4_en.html

15   Regional Policy

Though it always had its pockets of poverty, only with the admission of Ireland did the EC accept its first member state that could not be classed as industrialised, developed, and relatively well off. Since then, the growth to 15 members has included the admission of three more relatively poor countries – Spain, Portugal and Greece – whilst the planned enlargement to the east will transform the EU into a Union of 20+ countries on all sorts of income levels.

Looked at nation-by-nation, the Union does appear to have experienced a certain convergence between rich and poor in recent times, with the average income in the four poorest member states rising from two-thirds to three-quarters of the EU average in the eleven years up to 1996. The best performer of all has been Ireland, where per capita GDP increased from 64 per cent of the Community average between 1983 and 1995. A regional analysis over the 1986–96 period gives a quite different picture, however, with income in the poorest 25 regions rising by very little – from 53 per cent of the EU average to 55. Income disparities everywhere, in rich and poor regions and member states, have widened, with poverty and social exclusion rocketing and its social effects becoming ever more visible, especially in the streets of Europe's cities.[1]

It was in response to fears of just such developments that the Single European Act gave the European Union's institutions the legal competence to create a regional policy. Though it was never a major feature of the pro-integration propaganda barrage, the fact that the drive to complete the single market might actually increase regional disparities had long been quietly accepted, and it was felt necessary to establish a mechanism allowing for the transfer of relatively large amounts of money between different regions of the Community. This was controversial, as it would increase the degree to which taxpayers in the rich member states were asked to subsidise people in poorer areas. The removal of remaining barriers to the movement of goods, services and capital, however – and in particular the last of these – could, it was feared, lead to greater concentrations of wealth in areas already well favoured for such things as transport and financial infrastructure. In addition, the restructuring of European industry which would result from the completion of the single EC market, though its precise form might be hard to predict, would inevitably mean that some regional economies would see their traditional industries disrupted and would need to be helped through a period of transition in which they sought new means of earning their living. Finally, the single market would require certain countries, in most cases the poorer ones, to invest in expensive improvements to meet such demands as higher environmental standards. In 1988, following the ratification of the SEA by all of the member states, the European Council agreed a package, known as Delors I after the then President of the Commisssion, which foresaw a doubling by 1993 of the total available to the Structural Funds.[2]

With Maastricht, and the further deepening of integration in the form of Economic and Monetary Union, a new instrument, the Cohesion Fund, was added to the Structural Funds.[3] The Cohesion Fund was designed to assist only the very poorest regions and was available only to the 'poor four': Greece, Portugal, Spain and Ireland.

A further reform followed: the plan for the period 1994–99 aimed to give the Structural Funds more coherence, to increase their effectiveness as a means of combating unemployment and regional disparities of wealth. The revamped funds would also pay greater attention to environmental questions, or so we were promised, and to gender equality. Funding was increased following a new set of proposals from the Commission (Delors II), and 30b ECUs reserved for the period 1994–99. This was less than the Commission had proposed, however; it represents a compromise with a body of opinion within the member states (with the British Tories the least enthusiastic about this latest bout of integrationism but by no means isolated in their position) which was beginning to think that things had gone far enough. By 1999, structural-fund spending amounted to 36 per cent of the total EU budget, the second greatest share after the CAP.[4]

Generally speaking, the Structural Funds do not supply 100 per cent of the cash needed to finance a project. Payments are made according to what is loosely called 'matching': a member state government or other public or private institution invests in a project and the money is matched by a payment from the Structural Funds. The division of financial responsibility depends upon the particular Fund and the criteria under which the money has been allocated. The 'single programming document', whereby member states would produce a unified and coherent plan for the funds, then to be approved by the Commission and Council, was introduced in 1994 as part of a package of reforms designed to make the funds more effective and 'additionality' respected.

Put simply, 'additionality' means that member states must use any Structural Fund money to finance projects which would not otherwise have gone ahead. Although the Funds are (with the exception of small schemes known as the Community Instruments) to some extent under the control of the Commission and Council, it is the member states who decide who actually gets the cash. This leaves open the possibility that they will simply use the Funds to pay for things which they would otherwise have financed from the general budget. The British Tory government did this more or less openly, believing, as they did, that there was no greater virtue than low state spending. The Tories also rightly estimated that the British people in any case were of the opinion, and with no little justification, that the country paid out far too much to Brussels and got far too little back. As well as the additionality problem, loose monitoring has led to a chronic problem of fraud and waste.

AGENDA 2000

The latest, quite far-reaching reform of the Structural Funds took place at the beginning of 2000 on the basis of an agreement which began life as part of the Commission's all-embracing planning document, *Agenda 2000*. The agreement aims to enhance the effectiveness of the Structural Funds by further concentrating spending. The budget for seven years is a total of 213b euros, including 18b earmarked for the Cohesion Fund. As well as improving the effectiveness of operations in the existing member states, the reform is designed to enable the Structural Funds to be extended to newly admitted countries.

A major aspect of the reform has been the reduction in the number of Objectives – the criteria determining how money is spent – from seven to three. The new Objectives are as follows:

- Objective 1 promotes the development and structural adjustment of regions whose average per capita GDP is below 75 per cent of the European Union average; remote regions (the French overseas *départements*, the Azores, Madeira and the Canary Islands); regions eligible under old Objective 6, which gave aid to very sparsely populated regions and was part of the deal when Austria, Finland and Sweden became members. Two-thirds of available money goes to Objective 1. Eligible areas cover almost a fifth of the total EU population.

- Objective 2 contributes to the economic and social conversion of regions in structural difficulties which are nevertheless ineligible under Objective 1: former industrial and declining rural and fishing areas. This also covers not far off a fifth of the total population, but slightly fewer than does Objective 1.
- Objective 3 gathers together all the measures for human resource development outside the regions eligible for Objective 1.[5]

THE EUROPEAN REGIONAL DEVELOPMENT FUND (ERDF)

The ERDF now provides assistance under the new Objectives 1 and 2, including the new Community Initiatives (see below). Within the areas eligible under these Objectives, the ERDF contributes towards financing the following measures:

- Investment to create and safeguard sustainable jobs.
- Investment in infrastructure (including TENs) which contributes, in regions covered by Objective 1, to development, structural adjustment and creation and maintenance of sustainable jobs, or, in all eligible regions, to diversification, revitalisation, improved access and regeneration of economic sites and industrial areas suffering from decline, depressed urban areas, rural areas and areas dependent on fisheries. Development of the endogenous potential by measures which support local development and employment initiatives and the activities of small and medium-sized enterprises; such assistance is aimed at services for enterprises, transfer of technology, development of financing instruments, direct aid to investment, provision of local infrastructure, and aid for structures providing neighbourhood services.
- Investment in education and health (Objective 1 areas only).
- Measures are in all cases expected to take into account the need to develop research and technological facilities including information technology, to protect the environment, and to promote equal opportunities between men and women and transnational, cross-border and interregional co-operation.[6]

THE COHESION FUND

The Cohesion Fund is intended to contribute to the strengthening of the economic and social cohesion of the European Union, in particular preparing the poorer member states to take part in EMU. In order to do so, they are required to cut budget deficits and restrict debt, and the Cohesion Fund is aimed at mitigating the effects of the necessary cuts in public expenditure. In other words, it is the sugar coating on the pill of what amounts to a Structural Adjustment Programme, IMF-style. Indeed, until the end of 1999 it worked in much the same way: if a member state's deficit was deemed 'excessive', it got no more Cohesion Fund money until it got back into line.

With the adoption by Greece of the Euro at the beginning of 2001, the Cohesion Fund's initial goal of equipping countries to join the euro-zone was achieved, as only three EU member states, all of them wealthy countries – Sweden, Denmark and the UK – continued to shun the single currency. However, the planned entry of a large number of new members will once again make this aspect of the Cohesion Fund necessary. Until that happens, only projects to develop transport infrastructure or improve the environment in Spain, Greece, Ireland or Portugal are eligible. Only these four countries are included, because the rules state that only member states whose Gross National Product is below 90 per cent of the EU average may receive Cohesion Fund money. Financial support may be provided for a project up to 80–85 per cent of total public expenditure, a much higher proportion than is generally available under the older Funds. The total budget for 1993–99 was 15b ECU.

To qualify for Cohesion Fund assistance, projects must

- have clearly demonstrated medium-term economic and social benefits;
- contribute to achieving Community objectives for the environment and/or TENs;
- contribute to agreed priorities set by the member state in question;
- be compatible with other Community policies and Structural Fund objectives.

Once a project has been approved and is under way, it is the responsibility of the member state to implement it, monitoring it according to an agreed timetable and budget, though the Commission also carries out checks.[7]

THE COMMUNITY INITIATIVES

The Community Initiatives (CIs) were set up in 1989 and, unlike the rest of the Structural Fund instruments are under the direct control of the Commission, which, under agreed guidelines, decides who gets how much money. In 1994 the CIs were reformed and guidelines issued which foresaw the operation of 13 initiatives at a cost in all of 13.45b euros. In 1995, a special programme for Northern Ireland, the Peace Initiative, was added.

Following the experience of this six-year period, the decision was taken to concentrate the funds into four larger CIs. The budget was reduced to 10.44 billion euros, representing 5.35 per cent of the total allocation for the Structural Funds (2000–06). Despite this reduction, concentration of course meant that each of the remaining funds was much larger than its predecessors, and, as the Employment CI had been, divided into different sections. The four funds now in operation are:

- Interreg III: cross-border, transnational, and interregional co-operation;
- Urban: regeneration of urban areas in crisis;
- Leader +: rural development;
- Equal: transnational co-operation to combat discrimination and inequalities in access to work.[8]

THE EUROPEAN AGRICULTURAL GUARANTEE AND GUIDANCE FUND (EAGGF)

The EAGGF is divided into a 'Guarantee Section' (expenditure arising from the common organisation of the markets and agricultural prices, rural development measures accompanying market support and rural measures outside Objective 1 regions, expenditure on certain veterinary measures and information measures relating to the CAP) and a 'Guidance Section' covering all other rural development expenditure including the Community Initiative, Leader. Eligible measures include those which improve the environment through changes in (or the maintenance of) agricultural practices (so-called agro-environmental measures), early retirement assistance for farmers, modernisation and diversification of farm holdings, the installation of young farmers, and forestry schemes.[9]

THE FINANCIAL INSTRUMENT FOR FISHERIES GUIDANCE (FIFG)

Given the enormous cuts in quotas announced in December 2000, hard times are coming to those areas dependent on fisheries, most of which were hardly prospering prior to this. FIFG is designed to help these areas, though if it has the same sort of success as the Common Fisheries Policy itself then we had better start saving up to send food parcels. FIFG's first priority is a sustainable balance between fisheries resources and their exploitation, a goal which may already be out of reach. It also seeks to help enterprises in the sector (including aquaculture, processing and marketing) to enhance their 'competitiveness'. Specifically, it may award grants towards:

- fleet renewal and modernisation of fishing vessels, in keeping with the CFP;
- adjustment of fishing capacities;
- development of small-scale coastal fisheries;
- socio-economic measures;
- protection of marine resources;
- aquaculture;
- improvement of fishing port facilities;
- processing and marketing;
- finding new market outlets;
- innovative (preferably transnational) actions;
- technical assistance.[10]

16 Industrial Policy and Energy

The European Union has no specific, systematic industrial policy in the way that it has a policy for, say, agriculture or transport. Instead, what might be termed an 'EU industrial policy' is in reality an amalgam of elements of other policies laid out in many different sections of the Treaties: the completion of the internal market (including competition policy), EMU, external trade, social and regional policies, research and development, and energy. In addition, many measures are taken under competences such as environmental policy where the legislative process involved is the co-decision procedure and votes at Council are by Qualified Majority: the adoption at the end of 2000 of a new directive on the deliberate release of genetically-modified organisms, which had tremendous implications for the burgeoning biotechnology industry, the approval of pharmaceutical trials on children under a new regulatory system, which affected the interests of the pharmaceutical industry (also adopted late in 2000), and the possibility of severe restrictions being placed on the manufacture and use of PVC (under discussion in 2001) are all recent examples of this.

In contrast to the picture which emerged when we looked at the environment or development policy, then, it can be seen that industrial policy is fully 'mainstreamed', in a sense by default: the interests being dealt with are simply too powerful to ignore. The likely beneficiaries of a sound development strategy or victims of one which is poorly designed or deliberately exploitative are men, women and children whose voices have few opportunities to make themselves heard in the world. The 'green' NGOs who lobby Brussels for effective laws to tackle urgent environmental problems have together not a hundredth of the resources that a single multinational corporation can bring to bear on blocking them. Thus, whilst development and the environment are quickly forgotten by commission personnel not specifically responsible for those areas, the needs of industry never are. The EU's major industrial policy goals run like a recurrent motif through every area of policy, bolstering some measures, undermining others, giving shape and coherence to what at first appears to be a chaotic and incoherent body of legislation, action programmes, communications, recommendations, papers white and green: the EU's true *raison d'être* can be found here, in its determination to enforce a competition policy designed to bring about a liberalised market where the sort of interventionist approach suggested by the term 'industrial policy' becomes impossible. Instead, industries must be 'restructured' and everything subordinated to the principle of 'competitiveness', otherwise known as profit.

The Single European Market project was carried out largely in the interests of big European firms. Not only did it increase their market access, offering opportunities to take advantage of economies of scale, it made it easier to relocate to the most advantageous areas, to specialise at different productive facilities, and to save money by outsourcing parts of their operations. Firms in the construction, transport and other sectors have also benefited directly from the programme of infrastructure investment part-financed and led by the EU's Structural Funds.

The success of the internal market process encouraged further steps in industrial policy, formulated initially in the Commission's 1990 White Paper, *Industrial Policy in an Open and Competitive Environment* (COM(90) 556) and then as part of the 1993 White Paper, *Growth, Competitiveness, Employment – the Challenges and Ways Forward into the 21st Century* (COM(93) 700) which laid the basis for a decade of developing employment strategies, and gave further impetus to the idea of unified transport, telecommunications and energy networks – TENs.[1]

ENERGY POLICY

The European Coal and Steel Community which preceded and laid the ground for the EEC, had security of energy supply as one of its principal concerns. At the same time as the European Economic Community was created by the Treaty of Rome, moreover, so was the European Atomic Energy Community (Euratom). These two facts alone serve to demonstrate the place that energy has always had in the hierarchy of EC/EU concerns.

This makes it somewhat surprising that, after three major revisions of the Treaty in less than 15 years, it still contains very little specifically about energy. As with industrial policy, however, this is more a sign of a sort of effortless, almost unconscious 'mainstreaming' than it is of indifference. In addition, however, some member states have been extremely reluctant to hand over too much competence and control over energy to the Union. Energy supply in most countries remains in social ownership and often under the direct control of the state. It is not only politically a highly sensitive area, but in economic terms a potentially highly contentious matter: national energy policy has always offered, whatever the actual structure of ownership, a means of underwriting the competitiveness of a country's industries. Cheap energy can be achieved by efficiency, but also by socialising costs: in other words, through government intervention in the form of subsidy or tax measures, resources can be transferred from other areas of the economy in order to lower energy costs for everyone. This is a lot to give up, especially when the ability to manipulate one's national currency to give a boost to competitiveness has been thrown away. In addition, the objective situation of each member state in relation to energy is enormously varied, depending on possession of carbon fuel reserves, the extent of investment in nuclear energy and the amount of public interest, positive and negative, in one or another energy source. For different reasons coal, oil, nuclear power and renewable energy sources are all capable of generating not just power but an emotional response amongst the public which, in some cases, translates into organised action.

EU energy policy, when it can overcome these barriers, is guided by the 1995 *White Paper on an Energy Policy for the European Union*[2] and the Multi-annual Framework Programme for actions in the energy sector, which covers the period 1998–2002. Unlike food, energy is not to be treated as a special case: it is expected to follow the same principles as other sectors, pursuing a fully integrated, open EU market and contributing its share to the thorough deregulation and liberalisation of this market. Any attempt to intervene to influence energy prices as part of a member state's national industrial policy would be contrary to the Union's competition policy and the state must do the absolute minimum, limiting its actions to what is, firstly, allowed by the Treaty of Rome and the body of laws based on it and, if that condition is met, restricting itself to measures strictly necessary to safeguard the public interest – for example, to protect consumers or the environment.

The Framework Programme is an attempt to co-ordinate a number of EU policies and actions with a bearing on the energy sector. These include endeavouring to maintain the proportionate contribution of coal to overall energy consumption figures whilst increasing those of natural gas and renewables (the latter to 15 per cent by 2010) and tightening up safety regulations governing the construction of new nuclear power stations. These aims are motivated partly by environmental concerns, in particular the commitment to reduce greenhouse gas production undertaken as part of the UN agreement on climate change. They are also taken in pursuit of a long-term commitment to reduce dependency on oil imports, though UK oil made a much greater contribution to achieving this goal than any conservation measures or the development of safe, clean and indigenous alternatives.

Each energy sector presents its own difficulties. Only the UK, Germany and Spain continue to produce coal in any significant quantities, and in the latter two countries production continues only as a result of heavy subsidies. Imported coal is much cheaper, but curtailing subsidies would not only create unemployment but increase dependence on external sources. Most oil must continue to be imported, so that the EU encourages substitution of other fuels and exploration in search of new sources, as well as encouraging diversification of trading partners to safeguard against disruption of supply by political or other problems affecting one oil-producing country or group of countries. (Member states are also obliged to maintain a reserve equivalent to 90 days' consumption on the basis of the previous year's figures.)

Nuclear energy remains unpopular, its cover having been blown at Chernobyl and by hundreds of lesser accidents since. It also defies the normal rules of EU conduct by being economically untenable without heavy public subsidy. The EU has no harmonised safety standards or agreed maximum levels of discharges, and the different objective interests of the member states makes any common action difficult. Renewables are now taken seriously by the EU, which has just decided to allow member states to subsidise their development and hopes to raise their share of the market to 15 per cent by 2010. Conservation measures, which may hold greater potential for, for example, reducing greenhouse gas emissions than any plan to substitute one fuel for another, are given little emphasis in EU energy policy, except as a subject for research.[3]

TECHNOLOGY, RESEARCH AND DEVELOPMENT

Although research and development have been financed at supranational level in Western Europe since the establishment of the

European Coal and Steel Community in 1951, it was again the Single European Act which provided explicitly for Community competence. The Treaty empowers and obliges the Community to adopt a multi-annual research and development framework programme – in fact, simply putting on a more secure legal footing something which was already reality, as the First Framework Programme for Research and Development had already begun in 1994. Since Amsterdam, approval of this programme is by Qualified Majority. (A sub-programme for Euratom continues to require unanimous approval.) We are now on our fifth.

The object of these common programmes has been to co-ordinate national policies and research carried out directly in the name of the European Union. In this way duplicated efforts could be avoided, overall efficiency increased, resources pooled and costs lowered. Certain kinds of research, those with an inherently cross-border element – environment, public health, communications systems and transport telematics, to take a few examples – are seen as particularly appropriate for a multinational approach. By financing, and helping to determine the direction of, research, the EU hopes to help its member states and the corporations based in them to compete with Japanese and American industries with high research input. The EU's rival industrial superpowers each invests between 2.5 and 3 per cent of its GDP in research, with the average for EU member states being considerably lower, at under 2 per cent.

Research programmes may be 100 per cent financed, in which case they are carried out by the EU's own Joint Research Centre (JRC). The JRC is actually a complex of research facilities covering different scientific and technological areas and includes a controversial atomic energy research facility in the Netherlands as well as sites in Belgium, Italy, Germany and Spain. The EU also offers part-financing to other research projects which fit its aims, and sometimes makes grants to enable groups of researchers in different member states to co-ordinate their work.

The current (Fifth) Framework Programme for research and development runs from 1999 to 2002. The budget (which is much lower than was desired either by the Commission or the Parliament, and closer to the far more parsimonious sum which the member states, through the Council, were willing to part with, though it still represents a substantial real increase when compared to the Fourth Framework Programme) was fixed at ECU 14.96b of which ECU 1.26b was earmarked for nuclear power. At least 10 per cent of the total figure must be awarded to SMEs – small and medium-sized enterprises.

The Fifth Framework Programme does not only differ in size from the Fourth, it has also visibly changed with the times, placing emphasis on environmental questions and biotechnology, information and communication technology, and new materials. In the EU's view, the research effort which it is willing to fund must directly serve the interests of industry. In that respect, the Union's research and development policy is the handmaiden of its industrial policy, and the Framework Programmes can justly be seen as an element in that policy.[4]

17   Conclusion

My ambitions in writing this book were twofold. Firstly, I wanted to provide students with a basic guide to how the European Union functions. There are plenty of these around already, of course, but they are invariably written by people with a vested interest in spreading the integrationist gospel. This can make them quite painful to read, but it also distorts what they have to say. Certain arguments – such as that Qualified Majority Voting is inherently undemocratic, or that all sorts of feasible alternatives to this European Union exist – are deemed unworthy of consideration and simply ignored. For this writer, on the other hand, such questions go to the heart of the matter and, whatever side of the fence you eventually land on, no meaningful analysis of the EU is possible until they have been dealt with.

My second aim was to present a critique of the EU and its integrationist project which attempts to get right away from the question of nationalism and internationalism. I have written this book as an Englishman who lives in Belgium and works for an international organisation, representing a Dutch political party on the secretariat of the United Left Group in the European Parliament. Like most left-minded people of my generation I associate the Union Jack and flag of St George with fascist demonstrators. I believe nationalism to be the religion of fools and a major weapon in the armoury of charlatans. Yet I have no more time for 'European' nationalists than I do for any other kind. The sight of adults waving flags is generally an unedifying spectacle, whatever symbols appear on them, twelve gold stars included. On the other hand, the fact that decisions should be taken as close to home as possible, that the further away in distance and culture decision-making bodies become, the greater is the advantage to the rich lobbyist, these are sound reasons for defending the rights of national parliaments to do what they are supposed to do: express the will of the people. The fact that elected national bodies do this imperfectly is inarguable; but the European Parliament, the Committee of the Regions, the Economic and Social Committee – none of these expresses any will other than its own.

Culturally, nationalism is a dead end and we all deserve to have the world as our oyster. 'European' nationalism, as promoted by the self-styled 'pro-Europeans', is no different from any other kind. The EU is just part of a continent which is, in reality, merely a peninsula of the Eurasian landmass. The successful Norwegian campaign against accession had a slogan which captures this perfectly: *Europe is too small for us.*

Time and again we see reforms, carried out in the name of economic integrationism, which undermine political democracy; countries admitted to the Union following referenda in which the 'Yes' campaign's propaganda consists of lies, half-truths and irrelevancies; the militarisation of a 'Union' which is supposedly being constructed in the name of peace; the inflicting on people of an unwanted and bogus 'citizenship' over which none of the 'citizens' has been so much as consulted. Monetary union is sold to people in the most facile way, with no explanation as to what it really means and no admission of what it is really for. Successive summits attempt to convince us that a system which has kept unemployment high for decades can be transformed into a job creation machine, though of course we may have to give up a few social rights to achieve the promised land of full employment. A Community responsible for the Common Agricultural Policy, certainly the biggest single cause of environmental degradation in Western Europe since the war, now presents itself as a champion of the environment. And so on. Try as I might, I have been unable to identify a single policy area in which the Treaty of Rome has had a beneficial effect. Everything the EU does is either undesirable or could have been better achieved by other means.

The European Union is a technocratic project. That is to say that it is based on the premise that politicians can no longer be trusted with macro-economic policy. Neither they nor we, the people who elect them, understand it well enough. It must be left to specialists, to bankers, whom we are expected to believe are above the sectional interests which motivate the rest of us. The fact that the European Central Bank is answerable to no one, or that Qualified Majority Voting means that laws can be imposed on people against their express wishes and over the heads of their elected representatives are small prices to pay for greater 'efficiency'.

Technocracy has always done this, exploited the notorious 'inefficiency' of democracy to undermine people's confidence in themselves and their ability to run their own societies. If you agree that all decisions should be taken by 'experts', as far removed as possible from popular accountability, then the European Union of the Maastricht Treaty is precisely what you want. But if you believe in free co-operation between democratic nations then you should understand that that same Treaty removed whatever space the Treaty of Rome had allowed for such a system to develop.

Effective resistance is possible. In order to defend what is left of democracy, to create a genuine internationalism, and identify real alternatives for tackling the urgent problems facing all of our nations, we must first leave all the flags at home, forget about whose picture is on our money, and make a bonfire of all those national myths we were force-fed as children. Instead, look at the EU's policies and just how they are made. I have tried to make this book, with its bibliographies, a starting point for doing just that. Unless you happen to be the CEO of a multinational corporation, I believe that you will find that only one conclusion is possible.

THE EUROPEAN UNION: A SUMMARY OF THE CRITICISMS

In each chapter of this book you will find reasons, I believe, to question whether the EU in its present form is really the best approach to governance in the twenty-first century. Having spent the last 15 years working within one of its institutions (the European Parliament), I have seen nothing to disabuse me of the view that the integrationist project serves only one agenda – that of the multinational corporations (MNCs) whose growing hegemony of power at all levels threatens everything that has been gained by people in developed countries over the last two centuries: democratic rights and freedoms, economic security, the chance to live a dignified, productive, fulfilling life. This chance is now denied to a greater or lesser extent to growing numbers of people, whilst for most in the underdeveloped world they are further away than ever.

Numerous impulses fed into the original drive to establish the European Economic Community: the desire for a sustainable peace and the fear that Franco-German rivalry would once again destabilise the continent was certainly one of them. In the main, however, the Treaty of Rome set out to make Western Europe safe for capitalism, and in particular for the biggest corporations, which wanted a domestic market comparable to that available to their American rivals.

Since then, the power of corporations has grown, and that of other social forces diminished. This is reflected in the four major treaties – the Single European Act, and those of Maastricht, Amsterdam and Nice – which have carried integration ever further since the mid-1980s. Of course, other influences can be detected: the hesitancy of some member-state governments when it comes to handing over power to supra-national institutions; a cultural conservatism growing in part from the continuing power of Christianity (of various brands) in European social life; even, here and there, the aspirations of 'ordinary' men and women. The consistent theme, however, is that what's good for business is good for everyone, and what's good for business, of course, is to be able to make profit with as few restraints as possible – even where these restraints involve the wellbeing of the environment or the people and other beings which inhabit it.

The so-called Washington Consensus, which has dominated the theory and practice of big capital and its political servants for almost two decades, is that government expenditure as a proportion of GDP must be reduced, whilst the influence of the state gives way to the 'free play of market forces'. The corollaries of this idea, which lies at the heart of what is now known as 'neo-liberalism', are far-reaching. It means first of all that the state must withdraw from most spheres of economic activity. Nationalised industries must be sold off (in reality, most have been virtually given away). Where the market proves truly unable to provide a necessary service, you first question its necessity: thus, public transport no longer exists in huge stretches of rural and small-town America, because well, everyone has a car (which of course is not true) and if you do provide buses nobody uses them. Universal postal services are no longer needed because it makes more sense to ensure that everyone has email. And so on. If you do admit that a service which cannot possibly be profitable is nevertheless necessary, you subsidise a private firm to provide it, so that the firm's shareholders pick up the gains while the taxpayer covers the losses. And if people with more money can buy better food or a bigger car, why shouldn't they also spend their money on health care, or education, or having themselves or their children genetically modified so that they are brighter, taller, more beautiful than the rest?

Even to pose such questions demonstrates a moral bankruptcy and egotism which was once confined, at least publicly, to the fringes of the right, but which is now commonplace. The case for 'the market' is now rarely put – it is simply assumed; and with each successive revision of the Treaty, that assumption is carried further and deeper. Yet it rests, when examined, on the shakiest of foundations. Privatisation is necessary, we are told, because state-run enterprises are inefficient. There is in fact no weight of evidence in favour of this view, and none is regarded as necessary. A political viewpoint which once had to compete with others has the field to itself, transformed into a self-evident truth.

It is a 'truth' which guides the behaviour of the great institutions which run the system at global level – the IMF, World Bank, WTO and so on – and in huge 'regions': NAFTA for North America, Mercosur for Latin America, ASEAN for the Far East and the European Union for a growing area of Europe. Of these, the EU is by far the most highly developed, and the one whose agenda most closely resembles that of the WTO. Yet the World Trade Organisation is greeted with universal hostility by those on the left of politics or in the green movement, whilst resistance to the EU is seen, if only in the English-speaking world, as anti-internationalist and inward-looking.

Let me then finish by summarising why, as someone whose thinking and practice have been shaped by the traditions of the anti-capitalist left, I am also an opponent of this European Union.

Firstly, its institutions and their basis in the Treaty of Rome and its amending treaties, remove power ever further from the people. The policies pursued by member-state governments are increasingly constrained by EU rules which oblige them to impose a 'free market' logic on ever-broader areas of the economy. Decisions are taken by remote institutions – the European Central Bank, the European Commission, the Court of Justice – which are unelected and, with the partial exception of the Commission, not answerable to anyone who is elected. This means that the ballot box no longer offers a way to bring about any fundamental change in the direction of policy. The Council of Ministers, which at least represents elected governments, meets behind close doors and has the power, in more and more instances, to impose policies on peoples whose parliaments have never been given the chance to approve or disapprove them. The European Parliament is so remote an institution that a majority of the EU electorate does not bother to exercise its right to vote in elections to it. The idea, still current in anti-EU circles, that the EP is a talking shop with no real power is outdated. Yet the increase in its powers has done nothing to democratise the Union, because its growing powers have been gained at the expense not of the Union's unelected authorities but by further reducing those of the member states and their parliaments. Furthermore, its remoteness (and that of the Commission), in both geographic and cultural terms, from the lives of the vast majority of citizens tilts the balance away from popular institutions and democratic civil society and towards big corporations. It is the multinationals which have the resources to keep up a permanent lobbying clamour in Brussels and Strasbourg, a degree and style of pressure which is utterly disrespectful to the democratic process and ultimately subversive of it. From top to bottom the Commission and Parliament are imbued with such an elitist, technocratic world-view that they are not even aware of it. Despite valiant efforts from environmentalist, social and other NGOs, legislation which furthers the interests of the people rather than those of corporate capital almost never appears except as a result of one of two things: a crisis, such as the BSE scandal, which threatens to kill thousands of people and destroy hundreds of thousands of livelihoods, can provoke emergency action which may or may not include an effective remedy; or the need to mediate between competing national industries can lead to higher standards being imposed upon lagging countries. It would be overly pessimistic to say that sustained campaigning can never gain anything without one of these circumstances being present; and it would be wrong to pretend that national political institutions represent some ideal of democracy. What is certainly true, however, is that the EU has removed power from national institutions which can be understood, talked to and influenced, and handed it to a labyrinth of remote bodies in faraway places.

Secondly, these aspects of the Union have their effects across the board of policies and programmes for which it is responsible. Enlargement of the EU is not a means of bringing the two formerly divided halves of Europe into a harmonious whole; on the contrary, it is the latest of the spoils of what was proclaimed as the West's 'victory' in the Cold War. Democracy was, to say the least, much more in evidence to the west of the Iron Curtain than it was in the Eastern bloc. Until the dying days of the Soviet system, however, democracy was defined in large part as a political system which allowed people to choose between competing economic systems: market-based capitalism, state socialism, a mixed economy on social democratic lines, or some combination of these. Freedom of expression, of the press, of assembly and so on, were secondary to this, necessary because, clearly, political democracy cannot function without them. Now, however, these freedoms, together with a multi-party parliamentary system, are the very definition of democracy, which is the automatic and unvarying political adjunct of a free-market economy. Countries which lived in former times in the shadow of the USSR are now 'free' to join the European Union and adopt a particular, increasingly liberalised version of market capitalism as their economic system. Once in, their electorates will have no opportunity to change this system through constitutional means. Of course, they may stay outside the EU and the WTO, but if they do so no one will trade with them. They will therefore almost certainly opt to join, hoping that the corrupt, chaotic, nepotistic and gangsterish capitalism which has replaced repressive state socialism will somehow be modified by being 'in Europe'.

Meanwhile, to police the new Iron Curtain which will be erected when most of Central and Eastern Europe has been absorbed, the Union, this supposed guarantee of peace, steadily develops a military capability. If the system through which other policies are determined leaves much, from a democratic viewpoint, to be desired, the Common Foreign and Security Policy must take the prize. Based on an assumption that there exist such things as common European values, and that fundamental to these is the 'market economy', the CFSP is designed to allow the establishment of an EU armed force to protect the economic and political interests of the Union's most powerful member states. This is what is meant by 'stability', of course: a framework in which foreign corporations can make money. Together with the promotion of a vibrant, competitive arms industry this is the CFSP's purpose.

The EU is also about maintaining internal order, as is clear from a reading of the Treaty of Amsterdam and much, most of it supportive, that has been written since that Treaty was signed. The 'Third Pillar', tentatively introduced at Maastricht and reinforced in Amsterdam, represents a major inroad into what have been, after foreign policy, the most jealously guarded national competences: justice, the criminal law, immigration and refugee policy, and other aspects of what are tellingly known as 'home affairs'. Again, decisions are taken in an atmosphere of secrecy and elected assemblies at national and EU level excluded from the process. Bogus conceptions of citizenship are written into the Treaty, a meaningless Charter of Citizens' Rights agreed which imposes absolutely no new obligations on any of its signatories, and thus a blank cheque written to the future. What the Union will require of us now we are all its citizens is, of course, unknown, but when such decisions are taken we will have no involvement in them.

Probably the biggest single act of subversion of democracy committed in the name of the European Union has been the establishment of the single currency, the euro. The Maastricht Treaty's convergence criteria for admission to the single currency and the rules for participation exactly follow the Washington consensus, obliging member states to respect very narrow, arbitrarily established limits on public borrowing and debt, to submit to a common interest rate which may be utterly inimical to their actual needs, and to prioritise low inflation as a policy target: to follow, in other words, a particular idea of fiscal prudence. These rules are impervious to electoral change, and they are imposed by an unelected board of central bankers, one of the narrowest ruling elites in recent history. Before the advent of the euro, macro-economic policy was decided by elected politicians together with central banks which were, in most countries, directly answerable to them. Since the introduction of the single currency, it is determined by a Central Bank constitutionally defined as 'independent', one which those same elected politicians are forbidden by the Treaty even to seek to influence. Interesting choice of word, that 'independent'. In the context it means that it is able to operate entirely free of any constitutionally-sanctioned interference from the people or their elected representatives. The same can be said of Stalin, Hitler, or the Sultan of Brunei, yet dictators are never described as 'independent'.

The defence of this system is that ordinary people and politicians simply don't understand how the economy works and would get it all wrong. The great danger with this is that this attitude can equally be applied to other areas of policy, for what do non-specialists know about how to run a school or a hospital, about whether bio-technologies are safe, whether that new motorway is really needed or that forest really did have to be felled? Macro-economics is not in any obvious way a more difficult discipline than ecology, or health care economics, or plant biology; so why not apply the same logic to them and let experts decide everything?

The answer is that in democratic societies the people, and even the politicians, being ordinary mortals with limited knowledge and specialisms, cannot possibly decide every aspect of policy. What they can do, however, and what democracy, when it is genuine and functioning, allows them to do, is to establish policy goals. It is then the task of experts to work out how such goals can be achieved. It is precisely this right which the single currency, and the single internal market which it was designed, in part, to underpin, remove from the peoples of the member states.

Nor do the malign effects of this European Union stop at its borders. In its relationships with the rest of the world, the Union demonstrates a merely rhetorical awareness of the imbalance of power between North and South and the dangers this holds for both. In reality, it acts quite unrestrainedly in pursuit of the short-term interests of European owners of capital, and its highly selective commitment to free trade and its protectionism in defence of its member states' industries and agriculture have contributed much to the underdevelopment which has afflicted many of its poorer trading partners in the last three decades.

The EU's employment and social policies have been entirely ineffective in reducing either unemployment or the growing social divide, which interestingly has been most marked in what are seen as the most 'successful' economies, those in which growth has been most rapid and sustained, the Netherlands and Ireland. Its much-vaunted environmental policies have done little or nothing to redress the damage wrought by Common Agricultural, Transport and Fisheries Policies, the last of which may just take the prize for the most disastrous of EU measures, though competition is stiff.

Finally, the European Union distorts the natural desire of people to live in peace and co-operation with their neighbours. The integrationist answer to problems invariably involves ever greater transfer of power from nation state to Union institution. The method is to take an obvious statement – that environmental problems require cross-border solutions; that the globalised economy demands international co-operation if it is not to be controlled by the unrestrained, beyond-the-law actions of corporate cowboys; that a large market and a unified currency may hold advantages – and draw from it specious conclusions. Simply because we need an international approach to the problems facing humanity in the twenty-first century does not mean that *this* international approach, this European Union, a single currency based on discredited and extreme monetarist principles, a political system which seems almost designed to maximise corruption and the hegemony of wealthy elites, is the only or best form of international co-operation on offer.

If we are to develop genuinely international institutions which enable co-operation to take place whilst preserving the democratic rights of the peoples of different nations, then we must set about a root-and-branch re-examination and reconstruction of global governance. What cannot be reformed should be discarded, and what can be put to the service of the people should be reformed. In common with the WTO, the IMF, NATO and other instruments of globalised power, the European Union in its present form is an obstacle to real co-operation across borders of language, culture and history. Its likely result is an ever-growing divide between those who exercise power and those who must suffer the consequences of decisions taken by this elite. Though this may be the intention of some involved in the integrationist project, they are unlikely to enjoy the consequences. People denied peaceful means to bring about change can become apathetic, but sometimes they react in quite a different way. As anyone who has witnessed the recent history of Europe should know, they have even been known to dissolve long-standing Unions, reject the counsel of technocrats, and tear down walls.

Notes

2 THE TREATIES

1. Competence: the legal right to take action in a particular policy area.
2. Integrationism: belief in the further integration of European economy and society.
3. *The Amsterdam Treaty: A Comprehensive Guide*, Introduction, http://europa.eu.int/scadplus/leg/en/lvb/a09000.htm
4. Interview with Patricia McKenna, MEP, *Spectre* No. 5, Winter 1998, p. 6.

3 AND 4   THE INSTITUTIONS/HOW THE EUROPEAN UNION MAKES LAW

1. All quotes are from the Treaty of Nice. At the time of writing only a provisional text was available, at http://europa.eu.int/

5   ENLARGEMENT

1. European Commission.
2. See report at http://www.cnn.com/2000/WORLD/europe/09/05/germany.EU/.
3. European Commission, *Report on Progress Towards Accession by Each of the Candidate Countries*, November 8, 2000, \\Epades\Public\greffe2000\com\2000\com(2000)0700.
4. European Commission, ibid.
5. European Commission, ibid.
6. European Commission, ibid.
7. European Commission, ibid.
8. European Commission, ibid.

6   THE COMMON FOREIGN AND SECURITY POLICY

1. *Consolidated Version of the Treaty on European Union*, http://europa.eu.int/eur-lex/en/treaties/dat/eu_cons_treaty_en.pdf.
2. Paticia McKenna, *The Amsterdam Treaty: The Road to an Undemocratic and Military Superstate* at http://www.greenparty.ie/gpinteractive/amsterdam/defence.htm.
3. Bangemann is quoted in Patricia McKenna, MEP, ibid.; see also the BBC report on mergers in the defence industry at http://news6.thdo.bbc.co.uk/low/english/business/newsid_38000/38165.stm. The tone is summed up in this reported comment from Britain's defence minister: 'According to

the British Defence Secretary, George Robertson, Europe's defence industry might otherwise be wiped out by the Americans.

He said the message was "Rationalise or die – it's as blunt as that."

Defence contracts have been becoming more internationalised in recent years to share the huge costs of research and development. But what is envisaged is more radical than that.'

Britain, France and Germany account for 90 per cent of Europe's defence industry. The joint agreement by the three governments gives the nod to defence companies to merge formally. The timetable is short.'

4. Title V of the EU Treaty (CFSP), also known as the 'second pillar', contains the provisions establishing a common foreign and security policy. It comprises Articles 11 to 28. See http://europa.eu.int/scadplus/leg/en/lvb/a19000.htm.

5. Ibid.

6. *Conclusions of the European Council*, Cologne, 3–4 June 1999. http://www.europarl.eu.int/summits/kol1_en.htm#V. The two annexes *European Council Declaration on Strengthening the Common European Policy on Security and Defence*, and *European Council Declaration on Kosovo* contain the important developments in the CFSP.

7. Official CFSP website at http://ue.eu.int/pesc/pres.asp?lang=en.

8. Ibid.; and http://europa.eu.int/scadplus/leg/en/lvb/a19000.htm.

9. Official CFSP website at http://ue.eu.int/pesc/pres.asp?lang=en.

7   CITIZENSHIP, JUSTICE AND HOME AFFAIRS

1. 'The European Ombudsman is appointed by the European Parliament after each election for the duration of Parliament's term of office. He [*sic*] is empowered to receive complaints from any citizen of the Union or any natural or legal person residing in a Member State concerning instances of maladministration in the activities of the Community institutions or bodies (with the exception of the Court of Justice and the Court of First Instance). Where the Ombudsman establishes an instance of maladministration he refers the matter to the institution concerned, conducts an investigation, seeks a solution to redress the problem and, if necessary, submits draft recommendations to which the institution is required to reply in the form of a detailed report within three months. He submits a report to the European Parliament at the end of each annual session.' http://europa.eu.int/scadplus/leg/en/cig/g4000o.htm#o1.

2. Treaty of Amsterdam, Preamble, http://www.fletcher.tufts.edu/multi/texts/eucons.txt.

3. See the conclusions of the European Council, Cologne, 3–4 June 1999 at http://www.europarl.eu.int/summits/kol1_en.htm#V.

4. Draft Charter and European Parliament comment at http://www.europarl.eu.int/charter/default_en.htm; see also *Communication from the Commission on the Legal Nature of the Charter of Fundamental Rights of the European Union* at http://www.ecas.org/events/BRUN.htm.

5. The Schengen system, named after the Luxembourg village where the accord was signed in 1985, was made necessary by the reluctance of certain member states, notably the UK and Denmark, to participate in the development of a common system for the control of immigration or the treatment of asylum seekers. Such a system was clearly necessary if freedom of movement were to be fully realised (so that a foreigner arriving in one member state could move freely through all of them) and border controls done away with. Though this may sound a worthy goal, the agreement was widely criticised for its restrictive attitude and contribution to a 'fortress Europe' mentality. Because the agreement was outside the legal framework of the EC, unanimity always applied, meaning that it was generally necessary to bring everything down to the lowest common denominator in order to persuade the least foreigner-friendly government to sign. With some modifications, Schengen was incorporated into the EU Treaty at Amsterdam, and continues to attract criticism. The entire text of the original Schengen agreement is downloadable from http://spjelkavik.priv.no/henning/ifi/schengen.html.
6. See *European Parliament Fact Sheet: Justice and Home Affairs: General Aspects* at http://www.europarl.eu.int/factsheets/4_11_1_en.htm; and the numerous reports on Europol on the website of *Fortress Europe Circular Letter* , http://www.fecl.org/.
7. See Human Rights Watch World Report 1998: the Right to Asylum in the European Union, at http://www.hrw.org/hrw/worldreport/Helsinki-28.htm.
8. For an explanation of the Dublin Convention, as well as some general comment on the issues involved, see the European Parliament Fact Sheet Freedom of Movement, http://www.europarl.eu.int/factsheets/2_3_0_en.htm.

8   THE EURO

1. Jeremy Nilboer, Director of the European Foundation, quoted this in a speech to the Political Action Group for Europe, 23/5/99, on 'The pros and cons of Economic and Monetary Union'. The full text of this interesting speech is at http://www.bullen.demon.co.uk/nieboer.htm. Nilboer also quotes the following, from Hans Tietmeyer, President of the Bundesbank (German Central Bank): 'A European currency will lead to member states transferring their Sovereignty over financial and wage policy and in monetary affairs ... It is an illusion to think that states can hold on to their authority over taxation policies.' And then Commission head Jacques Santer: 'The realisation ... of the Economic and Currency Union is not possible without a political union.'
2. See Chapter 11 for more on this problem.
3. '58 per cent (end of 1999: 60 per cent) of Europeans support the introduction of the single currency, the euro, whilst 33 per cent (1 per cent up on the preceding six months) are against it. The euro enjoys 81 per cent support in Italy, 76 per cent in Luxembourg and Belgium and 75 per cent in Spain; this contrasts with only 22 per cent in the United

Kingdom and 38 per cent in Sweden. Among the countries in the euro zone, the level of support is well above the average for all 15 Member States.' Eurobarometer No. 53 July, 2000, http://europa.eu.int/comm/ dg10/epo/eb/eb53/highlights.html; additional statistics from official Commission source at http://europa.eu.int/comm/dg10/epo/ eb/eb53/ highlights.html.
4. Jeremy Nilboer 'The pros and cons of Economic and Monetary Union', http://www.bullen.demon.co.uk/nieboer.htm.
5. Technical details of the euro and EMU are taken direct from the Treaty on European Union (Maastricht Treaty) or from the four European Parliament Factsheets on the subject at http://www.europarl.eu.int/ factsheets/default_en.htm#5.

9   THE INTERNAL MARKET

1. Completing the Internal Market: White Paper from the Commission to the European Council (Milan, 28–29 June 1985) COM(85) 310.
2 The Cassis ruling, with a summary, can be found at http://www.fs.dk/ uk/acts/eu/efd_cauk.htm. A slightly lengthier discussion than there is room for here is at http://www.american.edu/ted/CASSIS.HTM. On the ECJ's ruling on the importing of beer to Germany, see http://www.beerchurch.com/reinheitsgebot.htm; for more on the ups and downs of the Danish bottle law, see http://www.american.edu/ projects/mandala/TED/DANISH.HTM.
3. See *European Parliament Fact Sheet: Principles and Completion of the Internal Market* at http://www.europarl.eu.int/factsheets/3_1_0_en.htm.
4. See http://www.mq.edu.au/PubRel/macquest/sciences2.htm. Catalytic converters are hard to maintain, transferring responsibility from manufacturer to consumer; and their effectiveness is hard to regulate. Failure to do so is of course the fault of government, law enforcers, etc. Everything is someone else's fault, never the manufacturer's, who has done his best, poor chap.
5. The full text of the directive is at http://www.europa.eu.int/eur-lex/en/lif/dat/1988/en_388L0361.html.
6. *Consolidated Version of the Treaty on European Union*, http://europa.eu.int/ eur-lex/en/treaties/dat/eu_cons_treaty_en.pdf.

10   EXTERNAL ECONOMIC RELATIONS

1. See Charles E. Hanrahan, *The U.S.–European Union Banana Dispute*, (CRS Issue Brief for Congress, Dec.1999) at http://www.cnie.org/nle/econ-39.html.
2. 'The EU and the US are the world's most important traders. The EU's share in total world trade (excluding intra-EU trade) amounted to 18.5 per cent in 1998 (19.2 per cent for exports and 17.7 per cent for imports); with the share of the US also amounting to 18.5 per cent (15.9 per cent

for exports and 20.7 per cent for imports). Taking only bilateral EU–US trade, it represents more than 7.1 per cent of total world trade. This is equal to the share of US–Canada bilateral trade. Trade between the US and Japan represented 4.2 per cent of total world trade in 1998.'
Source: *EU–US Trade and Biotechnology* on About.com at http://environ-ment.about.com/newsissues/environment/library/weekly/colorbook/blb iotech6b.htm?rnk=r1&terms=bilateral+EU-US+Trade.

3. A full list of countries which are involved in any sort of institutionalised co-operation with the EU, with links to each, is at http://www.euforic.org/resource/en/place.htm.

4. Commission website, http://europa.eu.int/comm/external_relations/.

11   EMPLOYMENT AND SOCIAL POLICY

1. http://europa.eu.int/comm/employment_social/general/com00–379/com379_en.pdf.

2. See Annex 1 of the Social Policy Agenda at http://europa.eu.int/comm/employment_social/general/com00–379/com379_en.pdf.

3. Jennie James 'Staying Put: For many Europeans there's no place like home', *Time Europe*, 8 May 2000, vol.155, 18 posted at http://www.time.com/time/europe/magazine/2000/0508/moving.html; see also the Commission *Action Plan for the Free Movement of Workers* at http://europa.eu.int/scadplus/leg/en/lvb/l32027.htm; and the discussion of freedom of movement in Chapter 7, and the internal market in Chapter 9.

4. The Eures website is at http://europa.eu.int/comm/employment_social/elm/eures/en/about/index.htm.

5. See the Commission's Education–Training–Youth website at http://europa.eu.int/scadplus/leg/en/s19000.htm#DIPLOMES.

6. See *Spectre* No. 1, Spring 1997, 'The Euro: First step towards a Europe where democracy is in the past tense' (Editorial comment); see also Chapter 8.

7. Melvyn Krauss, *The Euro and Europe's Welfare State, or How the Euro Will Save Europe* (June 2000),posted at http://www.project-syndicate.cz/docs/columns/Krauss2000July.asp.

8. *White Paper On Growth, Competitiveness, and Employment: The Challenges and Ways Forward into the 21st Century* COM(93) 700 final, 5 December 1993, posted at http://europa.eu.int/en/record/white/c93700/contents.html.

9. *European Social Policy – A Way Forward for the Union – A White Paper*, COM(94) 333, posted at http://europa.eu.int/comm/off/white/index_en.htm#1994.

10. 'Employability' is particularly popular, containing as it does the impli-cation that the unemployed are to blame for their own condition: they simply aren't employable enough; see, for example, the European Employment Strategy website at http://europa.eu.int/comm/employment_social/empl&esf/ees_en.htm.

11. 'The United States has been conducting a great economic experiment. It involves keeping unemployment rates at a historic low, over a long

period. The results are in: Sustained low unemployment achieves the good results its advocates have always claimed it would. Not only that: We've kept unemployment low without experiencing an upsurge of inflation.' E. J. Dionne 'JOBS WORK: The best social policy', *Commonweal*, 18 June 1999; Vicente Navarro, ' "Eurosclerosis" versus US dynamism' and Theodore Pelagidis 'European unemployment: myths and realities', *Challenge: The Magazine of Economic Affairs*, July–August 1998 are interesting discussions of this idea, from a more hostile viewpoint.

12. Stephen Hughes 'How to put Europe back to work', *New Statesman*, 29 November 1996.

13. Is there a new economy? First report on the OECD growth project at http://www.oecd.org/subject/growth/new_eco.pdf gives the US, Australia and Ireland (relatively deregulated labour markets) but also Denmark, the Netherlands and Norway (relatively regulated labour markets) as the countries which experienced the highest growth during the 1990s, also indicating that each was good at 'releasing human resources'. There is no obvious correlation between these six countries, though all except Ireland were extremely rich to start with, which might just have helped.

14. The report is at http://europa.eu.int/comm/employment_social/empl&esf/Emplpack/En/jointreport_en.pdf.

15. See European Commission Regional Policy Directorate General website at http://www.inforegio.cec.eu.int/wbover/overcon/oco2a_en.htm.

16. *European Parliament Fact Sheet: Health and Safety at Work*, http://www.europarl.eu.int/factsheets/default_en.htm.

17. For a complete list of health and safety at work legislative measures taken by the EC/EU, with links to full texts, go to http://europa.eu.int/eur-lex/en/lif/reg/en_register_05202010.html.

18. See the Commission health and safety website at http://europa.eu.int/comm/employment_social/h&s/index_en.htm.

19. European Agency for Health and Safety at Work, http://europe.osha.eu.int/.

20. See European Women's Lobby 'The Situation of Women in the EU' in *Spectre* No. 10, Summer 2000, at http://www.spectrezine.org/europe/womeninu.html, and Anita Cullberg, 'Gender is Negotiable: Still Some Way to Go for Swedish Women', *Spectre* No. 10, Summer 2000 at http://www.spectrezine.org/europe/womeninsweden.html.

21. Directive 75/117 of 10 February 1975.

22. All of these measures can be found in full on the EU's Community Legislation in Force (Lex) website. However, unlike health and safety measures (see above) gender issues are not categorised separately. To find a gender-related piece of legislation go to the social policy listing at http://europa.eu.int/eur-lex/en/lif/ind/en_analytical_index_05.html and follow the link to the category in which it will fall, depending on its content.

23. The ECJ ruling of 17 October 1995, Kalanke, C-450/93 held that positive action policy on recruitment and promotion contravened the 1976 Directive on equal treatment.

24   See the Commission's Education and Culture website at http://europa.eu.int/comm/dgs/education_culture/educ/index_en.html; and the (at time of writing, however, in overdue need of an update) *European Parliament Fact Sheet: Education, Vocational Training and Youth Policy* at http://www.europarl.eu.int/factsheets/4_16_0_en.htm.

25. See Commission Social Affairs Directorate General website at http://europa.eu.int/comm/employment_social/esf2000/glossary-en.htm.

26. See the Commission's Education-Training-Youth website at http://europa.eu.int/scadplus/leg/en/s19000.htm#.

27. See European Commission Directorate General for Social Affairs and Employment website at http://europa.eu.int/comm/employment_social/esf2000/glossary-en.htm; *Introducing the ESF,* http://europa.eu.int/comm/employment_social/esf2000/introduction-en.htm; and *Agenda 2000: For a Stronger and Wider Union,* http://europa.eu.int/scadplus/leg/en/s60000.htm.

12   THE ENVIRONMENT

1. See EIA website at http://europa.eu.int/comm/environment/eia/.
2. The consolidated Treaties, incorporating the Amsterdam Treaty's amendments, is at http://europa.eu.int/eur-lex/en/treaties/index.html.
3. Ibid.
4. Programme details at http://europa.eu.int/comm/environment/actionpr.htm.
5. *European Parliament Fact Sheet: Environmental Policy: General Principles.*
6. http://europa.eu.int/comm/environment/newprg/.
7. *European Parliament Fact Sheet: Public Health.*

13   THE COMMON AGRICULTURAL POLICY AND COMMON FISHERIES POLICY

1. *Consolidated Version of the European Union Treaties,* Official Journal C 340, 10.11.1997, pp. 173–308 posted at http://europa.eu.int/eur-lex/en/treaties/dat/ec_cons_treaty_en.pdf.
2. *Daily Telegraph* – parliamentary report 26/11/99.
3. The value of French farm land, for example, has fallen two-thirds since the mid-1970s; see 'Europe's disastrous Common Agricultural Policy' at http://www.ncpa.org/pi/internat/pd081000e.html; see also the (UK) National Farmers' Union (NFU) *Crisis in Farming: The Facts,* http://www.nfu.org.uk/crisis.asp.
4. See European Commission DG Fisheries website at http://europa.eu.int/comm/fisheries/policy_en.htm).
5. See 'Overfishing Cod,' *New Scientist,* 8 February 1997 at http://dhushara.tripod.com/book/diversit/extra/cod/cod.htm.

14   TRANSPORT

1. European Commission Directorate General for Transport and Energy, *Towards Sustainable Mobility* at http://europa.eu.int/comm/transport/themes/mobility/english/sm_4_en.html.
2. The Commission's action programme 1998–2004 for transport, http://europa.eu.int/en/comm/dg07/ctp_action_prog/ctpen.htm.
3. These papers are available at http://www.cordis.lu/transport/src/public1.htm.
4. The Commission's action programme 1998–2004 for transport, http://europa.eu.int/en/comm/dg07/ctp_action_ prog/ctpen.htm.
5. Nicholas Moussis, *Handbook of the European Union*, 4th Edn p. 251 (European Study Service, 1997).
6. See 'The Two Faces of EU Transport Policies', *Corporate Europe Observer* No. 3, http://www.xs4all.nl/~ceo/observer3/general.html#faces.
7. *Transport & Environment Bulletin*, October 1998.
. The Commission's outline of TENs is at http://europa.eu.int/en/agenda/ten/ten.html; see also 'The Two Faces of EU Transport Policies', *Corporate Europe Observatory* No. 3, http://www.xs4all.nl/~ceo/observer3/general.html#faces.

15   REGIONAL POLICY

1. European Commission Directorate General for Regional Policy, *The European Union: Cohesion and Disparities* at http://www.inforegio.cec.eu.int/wbover/overcon/oco2a_en.htm.
2. Ibid.
3. The Structural Funds are the European Regional Development Fund (ERDF), the European Social Fund (ESF) described in Chapter 11, the 'Guidance' Section of the European Agriculture Guidance and Guarantee Fund (EAGGF), and the Financial Instrument for Fisheries Guidance.
4. European Commission Directorate General for Regional Policy, op. cit.
5. European Commission, *Agenda 2000: Structural Funds Reform*, http://europa.eu.int/scadplus/leg/en/lvb/l60013.htm.
6. Ibid.
7. Details of how the money was spent are at http://www.inforegio.org/wbpro/procf/Fund/prcf4_en.htm.
   For more detailed information, including a list of projects, go to the Cohesion Fund website at http://www.inforegio.org/wbpro/procf/cf_en.htm; the Regional Policy Directorate General of the Commission's website is at http://www.inforegio.org/wbover/over_en.htm.
8. For more details go to http://www.inforegio.org/wbpro/PRORD/prordc/prdc4_en.htm.
9. http://www.inforegio.org/wbover/over_en.htm.
10. Ibid.

16   INDUSTRIAL POLICY AND ENERGY

1. The 1990 White Paper is not available on line, at least not through the official website where White Papers are normally found. The 1993 White Paper is at http://europa.eu.int/en/record/white/c93700/contents.html.
2. http://europa.eu.int/en/comm/dg17/whitepap.htm.
3. See the Green Paper *Towards a European Strategy for the Security of Energy Supply* (2000), http://europa.eu.int/comm/dgs/energy_transport/index_en.html.
4. See the website of the Directorate General for Research, http://europa.eu.int/comm/dgs/research/index_en.html.

Recommended Reading

1   INTRODUCTION

Books

Timothy Bainbridge and Anthony Teasdale, *The Penguin Companion to European Union* (Penguin,1998).
David Butler and Martin Westlake, *British Politics and the European Elections1999* (Macmillan, 2000).
Alan J. Day, *Directory of European Union Political Parties* (John Harper, 2000).
Martin Holmes (ed.), *The Eurosceptical Reader* (Macmillan, 1996).
Rodney Leach, *Europe: A Concise Encylopedia of the European Union from Aachen to Zollverein* (Profile, 2000).
Dick Leonard, *Guide to the European Union* (Profile, 7th edn, 2000).
John McCormick, *Understanding the European Union: A Concise Introduction* (Macmillan, 1999).
Nicholas Mussis, *Handbook of the European Union* (European Study Service, 5th edn, 1998).
Anne Ramsey *European Union Information* (Association of Assistant Librarians, 2nd edn, 1997).
Alex Roney, *EC/EU Fact Book* (Kogan Page, 2000).
Alex Roney and Stanley Budd, *The European Union: A Guide Through the EU/EC Maze* (London; Kogan Page/Institute of Directors, 6th edn, 1998).

Websites, Papers, etc.

http://www.uflib.ufl.edu/docs/EUguide/eupubs.html. This University of Florida site offers links to a huge range of official and unofficial publications on EU affairs.

A collection of links to universities and private research organisations around the world that participate in the study of the European Union is at http://www.indiana.edu/~unionet/ academic.htm.

A comprehensive EU bibliography with links to other sites is provided at http://www.law.nyu.edu/library/foreign_intl/ european.html. www.europarl.ep.ec/dg4/factsheets/en/default.htm. Frequently updated 'fact sheets' from the European parliament on EU affairs.

http://www.cec.org.uk/. Most useful to students in the main not because of the information it contains, but because of its 'bibliography' (*EU Information Sources in the UK* and *Links*).

http://www.euro-know.org/dictionary/e.html. A concise and irreverent, but nevertheless informative, encyclopedia of the EU.

http://www.eurplace.org/grandtour/gt/documen/cronoen.html. A chronology
of the EC/EU.

http://www.europarl.eu.int/home/. European Parliament home page,
through which a wide range of official sources can be accessed.

http://eubasics.allmansland.com/index.html. Regularly updated straightforward guide to EU matters.

http://www.socio.ch/internat/geser1.htm. Contains the essay 'Why the EU
Cannot Succeed'; site also contains a very useful list of papers and other
resources on European Union affairs, with hypertext links.

2   THE TREATIES

Books

British Management Data Foundation, *The Treaty of Amsterdam in Perspective*
(BMDF, 1998).
Desmond Dinan, *Ever Closer Union: An Introduction to European Integration*
(Lynne Rienner Publishers, 1999).
Anthony Forster, *Britain and the Maastricht Negotiations* (Palgrave, 1999).
Christine Ingebritsen, *The Nordic States and European Unity* (Cornell UP, 1998).
P. Lynch, N. Neuwahl and W. Rees, *Reforming the European Union* (Longman,
2000).
John McCormick, *The European Union: Politics and Policies* (Westview Press,
1999).
Karlheinz Neunreither and Antje Wiener, *European Integration After Amsterdam*
(Oxford University Press, 2000).
Ben Rosamond, *Theories of European Integration* (Macmillan, 2000).
Larry Siedentop, *Democracy in Europe* (Penguin, 2000).
Teija Tiilikainen and Ib Damgaard Petersen, eds, *The Nordic Countries and the
EC* (Copenhagen Political Studies Press, 1993).

Websites, Papers, etc.

Dag Arne Christensen, 'The Left-wing opposition in Denmark, Norway and
Sweden: cases of Euro-phobia?', *West European Politics* 1996 19(3): 525–46.
Claus Dieter Ehlermann, *Differentation, Flexibility, Closer Co-operation: The New
Provisions of the Amsterdam Treaty* http://www.iue.it/RSC/WP-
Texts/ehlermann.html.
Jens Henrik Haahr, 'European integration and the left in Britain and
Denmark', *Journal of Common Market Studies*, 1992, 30(1): 77–100.
Patricia McKenna, MEP, 'The Amsterdam Treaty: the road to an undem-
ocratic and military superstate' at http://www.greenparty.ie/
gpinteractive/amsterdam/intro.htm.

Nikolaj Peterson, 'The Danish referendum on the Treaty of Amsterdam' (Bonn: Zentrum flr Europdische Integrationsforschung, Rheinische Friedrich-Wilhelms-Universitdt Bonn, 1998. p. 37 *ZEI Discussion Paper*, C 17).
Clare Smedley, 'The 1996 Inter-Governmental Conference: reviewing Maastricht and the European Project' at http://www.oneworld.org/aprodev/aproigc.htm.
Palle Svensson, 'The Danish yes to Maastricht and Edinburgh: the EC referendum of May 1993', *Scandinavian Political Studies* 1994 17(1): 69–82.

3 THE INSTITUTIONS

Books

Richard Corbett, Francis Jacobs and Michael Shackleton, *The European Parliament* (John Harper Publishing, 4th edn, 2000).
Renaud Dehousse, *The European Court of Justice* (Macmillan, 1998).
Justin Greenwood, *Representing Interests in the European Union* (Macmillan, 1997).
Fiona Hayes-Renshaw and Helen Wallace, *The Council of Ministers* (Macmillan, 1997).
Neil Nugent, *The European Commission* (Palgrave, 2000).
Neil Nugent (ed.), *At the Heart of the Union: Studies of the European Commission* (St Martin's Press, 2000).
Philippa Sherrington, *The Council of Ministers: Political Authority in the European Union* (Pinter, 2000).
Paul van Buitenen, *Blowing the Whistle* (London; Politico's Press, 2000).
Martin Westlake, *The Council of the European Union* (Cartermill; 1995).

Websites, Papers, etc.

You can access all of the official EU institutions and information services through a single gateway at http://europa.eu.int/index-en.htm.
Michael Nentwich and Gerda Falkner, *The Treaty of Amsterdam: Towards a New Institutional Balance* in EloP, Vol.1 No.15, 25/8/97 at http://www.eiop.or.at/eiop/texte/1997–015.htm.
Wolfgang Wessels and Udo Diedrichs, *A New Kind of Legitimacy for a New Kind of Parliament* in European Integration on-line Papers (EloP), Vol.1 No.6, 10/4/97 at http://eiop.or.at/eiop/texte/ 1997–006a.htm.

4 HOW THE EU MAKES LAW

Books

Erik Oddvar Eriksen and John Erik Fossum (eds), *Democracy in the European Union: Integration through Deliberation?* (Routledge, 2000).

Daniel Guégen, *A Practical Guide to the EU Labyrinth* (Editions Apogée: Collection Sésame Pour l'Europe, 4th edn, 2000).
Neill Nugent, *The Government and Politics of the European Union* (Macmillan, 1999).
Jo Shaw, *The Law of the European Union* (Palgrave, 2000).

Websites, Papers, etc.

http://www.eurim.org/cassidy.htm contains the *Eurim Guide to Decision-Making in the European Union* by Conservative Euro-MP Bryan Cassidy.

http://www.libraries.psu.edu/crsweb/docs/euquickm.htm gives a useful brief rundown on the role of each institution of the EU as well as a host of links and other invaluable information.

http://www.kub.nl/~dbi/english/instruct/eu/legislat.htm goes into a little more detail. Written for law students, this site gives a rundown on the legislative process and a brief case study. It also explains how to use EU publications and documents, and the status of each category of these.

EUR-Lex, at http://europa.eu.int/eur-lex/en/index.html is designed to keep you up to date on legislation in force in the European Union and new legislation as it is enacted.

Still more detail is on the Harvard University course notes site at http://www.law.harvard.edu/programs/JeanMonnet/course99w/Units/unit1toc.html.

The Bora Laskin Law Library has a guide to on-line resources on EU legal affairs, entitled *Selective Source Guides to Research in International Law: GUIDE II: THE EUROPEAN UNION – A Brief Guide to the Basic Print and Electronic Sources for Legislation, Case Law, and Secondary Material* at http://www.law-lib.utoronto.ca/resguide/eubrief.

http://www.law.smu.edu/library/resguide/eu.htm is a guide to researching EU law on line.

5   ENLARGEMENT

Books

Alice H. Amsden *et al.*, *The Market Meets Its Match : Restructuring the Economies of Eastern Europe* (Harvard University Press, 1998).
Laszlo Andor and Martin Summers, *Market Failure: Eastern Europe's 'Economic Miracle'* (Pluto Press, 1998).
Michael J. Baun, *A Wider Europe: The Process and Politics of European Union Enlargement* (Routledge and Littlefield, 2000).

Kate Hathaway and Dale E. Hathaway (eds), *Searching for Common Ground: European Union Enlargement and Agricultural Policy* (FAO, 1998).

Teresa Hayter, *Open Borders: The Case Against Immigration Controls* (Pluto Press, 2000).

Pierre-Henri Laurent and Marc Maresceau (eds), *The State of the European Union (Vol.4): Deepening and Widening* (Lynne Reinner, 1997).

Victoria Curzon Price, Alice Landau and Richard Whitman, *The Enlargement of the European Union: Issues and Strategies* (Routledge Studies in the European Economy, 1999).

Websites, Papers, etc.

Official reports on the status of each applicant in November, 1999 are available at Commission of the European Communities, *Report on Progress Towards Accession by Each of the Candidate Countries*, 8 November 2000, \\Epades\Public\greffe2000\com\2000\com<2000>0700p.6.

For more recent reports consult the enlargement websites of the EU institutions at http://www.europarl.ep.ec/enlargement/.

The European Commission's background briefings on enlargement can be found at http://www.cec.org.uk/pubs/bbrief/bb2598.htm.

The European Commission also offers a site with numerous links at http://europa.eu.int/comm/enlargement/index.htm.

http://www.mem.dk/aarhus-conference/newslet/articels/eurounio.htm gives an official view of the environmental implications of enlargement.

See http://stars.coe.fr/ta/ta97/erec1347.htm for the view of the Parliamentary Assembly of the Council of Europe.

European Union Enlargement: An SAIS Research Project, at http://www.eue.org/ http://www.euroguide.org/euroguide/subject-listing/enlargement.html contains a variety of resources on enlargement.

http://www.europarl.eu.int/enlargement contains a survey on public opinion in the applicant countries.

Per Capita GDP Below 75 per cent of EU Average in 48 Regions Out of 50, downloadable PDF format file posted at http://europa.eu.int/comm/ eurostat/datashop/print-catalogue/EN?catalogue=Eurostat&product=1– 18042000-EN-AP-EN; see other statistics indicative of degrees wealth and wellbeing at r.cade EU indicators website, http://www-rcade.dur.ac.uk/ ods/maps/country.html.

Hiroyuki Shinkai (ed.), Unicri Issues and Reports No. 10, *Combating Corruption in Central and Eastern Europe* available at http://www.unicri.it/html/ body_issues___reports_no__10.htm.

See the MINELRES directory of resources on minority situation and minority human rights, inter-ethnic conflicts, ethnic policies, migration and refugees flows and related problems of the transition period in Eastern and Central Europe at http://www.riga.lv for a thorough account of the problems in the region.

Nicholas Johnson *Poland and the European Union*, http://www.wonet.com.pl/outlook/pol_eu.html.

Timo MÄKELÄ (Head of Unit Directorate General XI 'Environment, Nuclear Safety and Civil Protection', European Commission) *Enlargement of the European Union Part of the 'Environment for Europe' Process* at http://www.mem.dk/aarhus-conference/newslet/articels/eurounio.htm.

An official Hungarian government view of relations between that country and the EU is at http://www.mfa.gov.hu/sajtoanyag/sajto51.htm.

One of the most useful sites is *Countdown, an Online Information, Documentation and Communication Centre on the European Union's Eastern Enlargement* at http://wiiwsv.wsr.ac.at/Countdown/.

The European Environmental Bureau newsletter *Metamorphosis* carries a regular 'Enlargement update'. The Bureau has a website at www.eeb.org.

On migration and east–west labour mobility, see Stephen J. H. Dearden, *Immigration Policy in the European Community*, Manchester Metropolitan University, DSA European Development Policy Study Group Discussion Paper No. 4, March 1997, http://www.euforic.org/dsa/dp4.htm.

Nancy Holstrom and Richard Smith, 'The necessity of gangster capitalism: primitive accumulation in Russia and China', (*Monthly Review*, Vol. 51, No. 9, February 2000).

'Comment: keeping up the pace in enlargement talks', *European Voice*, 16 November 2000 'Poised to take the plunge', *Financial Times*, 6 November 2000.

'Enlarged EU is priority for Swedes', *FT*, 2 January 2001.

6   THE COMMON FOREIGN AND SECURITY POLICY

Books

Per Gahrton, *The New EU After Amsterdam* (Green Group, European Parliament, 1997).
Terrence R. Guay, *At Arms' Length : The European Union and Europe's Defence Industry* (St Martin's Press, 1998).

Martin Holland (ed.), *Common Foreign and Security Policy: The Record and Reform* (Pinter, 1997).

Elfriede Regelsberge (ed.), *Foreign Policy of the European Union: From Epc to Cfsp and Beyond* (Lynne Riener Publishers, 1996).

Websites, Papers, etc.

You can read Title V of the Amsterdam Treaty for yourself at http://europa.eu.int/en/record/mt/title5.html.

A good brief introduction to the CFSP is at http://www.euro-know.org/dictionary/c.html#c3.

The official view is given in a pamphlet which can be found at http://europa.eu.int/comm/dg10/publications/brochures/move/relex/pesc/txt_en.html.

The pamphlet *How Does the EU Relate to the World?* puts the CFSP in the broader context of international relations, including development policy. It is posted at http://europa.eu.int/comm/dg10/publications/brochures/move/relex/qaworld/txt_en.html.

The 1996 European Commission White Paper, which amongst other things gives a run-down on each (then) member state's position regarding the CFSP, can be found at http://europa.eu.int/en/agenda/igc-home/eu-doc/parlment/peen2.htm.

An official Commission Communication on *Implementing the European Union Strategy on Defence-related Industries* (1997) is at http://europa.eu.int/comm/dg03/publicat/aerospac/com583e.htm.

The European Defence Industries Group has a website at http://www.edlg.org/.

An official WEU view, though a little outdated, is contained in a paper entitled *Europe and the Challenge of Proliferation* at http://www.weu.int/institute/chaillot/chai24e.htm.

A brief summary of highly critical views of recent developments in the CFSP is at http://www.kc3.co.uk/~dt/justice.htm#Army.

NATO's contribution in *NATO A to Z, Part 1: The Transformation of the Alliance: The European Security and Defence Identity* is at http://www.nato.int/docu/handbook/hb10800e.htm.

Irish Green Euro-MP Patricia McKenna's excellent, well-argued attack on the Amsterdam Treaty – particularly its implications for CFSP – cited more than once in the above chapter, was written for the NO campaign in the post-Treaty referendum. It can be found at http://www.greenparty.ie/

gpinteractive/amsterdam/intro.htm. McKenna covers much the same ground in her interview with *Spectre* (conducted by the author) in *Spectre* No. 5, Winter 1998, pp. 6–8.

Another oppositional piece is Graham Stewart *The Common Foreign and Security Policy*, http://www.keele.ac.uk/socs/ks40/cfsp.htm.

Leo Dreapir of the Campaign Against Euro-federalism shares some of McKenna's criticisms but adds others. See Leo Dreapir *EU Common Foreign and Security Policy: National Independence or Global War Policy?* (Discussion Pamphlet, Campaign Against Euro-federalism, 1999). CAEF has a website at www.poptel.org.uk/against-federalism.

Further material expressing a variety of views:
Helene Sjursen *The Common Foreign and Security Policy: An Emerging New Voice in International Politics?* (Arena Working papers, WP99/34) at http://www.nato.int/docu/handbook/hb10800e.htm.

Centre for European Security and Disarmament http://www.cesd.org/ (nb: this site was still under construction at time of writing).

Florika Fink-Hooijer, 'The Common Foreign and Security Policy of the European Union', *European Journal of International Law, Vol.5, No.2* posted at http://www.ejil.org/journal/Vol5/No2/art2.html.

And if that's not enough, you can consult a directory entirely devoted to the EU's external relations at http://dmoz.org/Society/Politics/European_Union/External_Relations/.

7   CITIZENSHIP, JUSTICE AND HOME AFFAIRS

Books

Stephen Hall, *Nationality, Migration Rights and Citizenship of the Union* (Kluwer Law International, 1995).
Catherine Hiskyns and Michael Newman, *Democratising the European Union* (Manchester UP, 2000).
Massimo La Torre (ed.), *European Citizenship: An Institutional Challenge* (Kluwer Law International, 1998).
Percy B. Lehning and Albert Weale (eds), *Citizenship, Democracy, and Justice in the New Europe* (Routledge, 1997).
Siofra O'Leary, *The Evolving Concept of Community Citizenship : From the Free Movement of Persons to Union Citizenship* (Kluwer Law International, 1997).
Larry Siedentop, *Democracy in Europe* (Penguin, 2000).
Michael Spencer, *States of Injustice : A Guide to Human Rights and Civil Liberties in the European Union* (Pluto, 1995).

Jens Magleby Srensen *et al*., (eds), *The Exclusive European Citizenship : The Case for Refugees and Immigrants in the European Union* (Avebury, 1996).

Albert Weale and Michael Nentwich (eds), *Political Theory and the European Union: Legitimacy, Constitutional Choice and Citizenship* (Routledge/European Centre For Policy Research, 1999).

Websites, Papers, etc.

The five European Parliament Fact Sheets on *Citizens' Europe* can be accessed through the index at http://www.europarl.eu.int/factsheets/default_en.htm#5.

The European Parliament's comment on the Charter of Fundamental Rights is at http://www.europarl.org.uk/EU%20Charter%20special/ txmain.htm. The site also contains a number of comments from the press regarding the Charter as adopted at Nice.

The Commission gives information on 'fundamental rights and freedoms' at http://europa.eu.int/abc/cit1_en.htm. *Communication from the Commission on the Legal Nature of the Charter of Fundamental Rights of the European Union* is at http://www.ecas.org/events/BRUN.htm.

Not bang up to date in the details but still offering a useful perspective from those who see a legally-binding charter of rights as the best way to preserve freedoms in the EU, the European Citizens Actions Service paper *European Citizenship: Giving Substance to Citizens' Europe in a Revised Treaty* is at http://www.eurplace.org/diba/citta/ecas.html.

Christiane Lemke 'Citizenship and European integration', *World Affairs*, Spring 1998, http://www.findarticles.com/cf_0/m2393/n4_v160/20461053/p1/article.jhtml?term=European+Union.

The *Irish Times* produced a thorough guide to the Amsterdam Treaty, with a section on Justice and Home Affairs, at http://www.ireland.com/special/treaty/treaty/chap8.htm.

Adrian Favell and Andrew Geddes, 'Immigration and European integration: new opportunities for transnational political mobilisation?', in Ruud Koopmans and Paul Statham (eds), *Challenging Immigration and Ethnic Relations Politics: Comparative European Perspectives* (Oxford UP, 2000).

http://www.statewatch.org/ 'monitoring the state and civil liberties in the European Union'.

8 THE EURO

Books

Mark Baimbridge *et al.*, *The Impact of the Euro: Debating Britain's Future* (St Martin's Press, 1999).

Noah Barkin *et al.* (eds), *EMU Explained: The Impact of the Euro* (Kogan Page, 1998). Jean Jacques Rosa, *Euro Error* (Algora, 1999).

Christian N. Chabot, *Understanding the Euro: The Clear and Concise Guide to the New Trans-European Currency*, (McGraw-Hill, 1998).

Jonathon Coppell *et al.* (eds), *EMU: Facts, Challenges and Myths* (OECD, 2000).

Kenneth Dyson, *The Politics of the Euro-Zone: Stability or Breakdown* (Oxford UP, 2000).

Malcolm Levitt and Christopher Lord, *Political Economy of Monetary Union* (Macmillan, 2000).

Jean-Victor Louis and Hajo Bronkhurst, (eds), *The Euro and European Integration* (Peter Lang, 1999).

Kathleen N. McNamara *The Currency of Ideas: Monetary Politics in the European Union* (Cornell UP, 1999).

Doug Nicholls, *The Euro: Bad For Trade Unions* (Congress for Democracy, 1999).

Thierry Vissol, *The Euro: Consequences for the Consumer and the Citizen* – extracts from the report of a European Commission working group on the subject (Kluwer Academic Publishing, 1999).

Websites, Papers, etc.

The European Central Bank's website is at http://www.ecb.int.

The four European Parliament Fact Sheets on the Euro can be accessed through the index at http://www.europarl.eu.int/factsheets/default_en.htm#5.

Wade through the propaganda to find up-to-date information on the Euro's performance at http://www.euro-information.com/.

Another official source is on the EU's official website in the US: *Everything You Need to Know about Europe's New Currency, the Euro* is at http://www.eurunion.org/magazine/eurospec.htm.

Links to sites expressing a wide variety of views and offering comprehensive information are at http://info.ex.ac.uk/~RDavies/arian/euro.html.

Finally, for a more detailed and technical bibliography, albeit one with a certain oppositional leaning, see http://www.euro-know.org/biblio.html#top.

9   THE INTERNAL MARKET

Books

Kenneth A. Armstrong and Simon J. Bulmer, *The Governance of the Single European Market* (St Martin's Press, 1998).

Edward Elgar, *The Evolution of the Single European Market* (Edward Elgar, 1997).

Bill Lucarelli, *The Origins and Evolution of the Single Market in Europe* (Ashgate, 1999).

Mario Monti *et al.*, *The Single Market and Tomorrow's Europe : A Progress Report from the European Commission* (Kogan Page, 1998).

Alan Philips and A. B. Philip, *The Single European Market* (Longman, 2000).

Websites, Papers, etc.

The European Parliament has produced a total of 14 *Fact Sheets* on different aspects of the Internal Market. These can be accessed through the index at http://www.europarl.eu.int/factsheets/default_en.htm#3.

The European Commission's internal market website is at http://europa.eu.int/comm/internal_market/en/index.htm.

Links to various EU resources on its competition policy, including all relevant legislative texts, are at http://europa.eu.int/pol/comp/index_en.htm.

The London office of the Commission has a guide to consumer policy which is 'mainstreamed', even if the policies themselves aren't: it takes a useful look at implications for other policy areas such as the CAP. Go to http://www.cec.org.uk/pubs/bbrief/bb3298.htm.

The European Union in the US official magazine *Europe* has a special section on competition policy. Go to http://www.eurunion.org/legislat/comweb.htm.

Try http://www.pitt.edu/~wwwes/sm.guide.html#www for useful links, including to bibliographies, and http://www.stile.lboro.ac.uk/~gyedb/STILE/t0000537.html for a more comprehensive list of websites.

A list of consumers' organisations internationally, including those concerned with the EU, with links to each is at http://www.vii.org/afica.htm.

A European Parliament Background Study, *Public Undertakings and Services in the European Union* (1997) is available in summary form, with a link to the full text, at http://www.europarl.eu.int/workingpapers/econ/w21/sum-toc_en.htm.

See British Green Euro-MP's press release of 17/11/00 'EU Commission threat to Britain's public services: the European Commission's GATS negotiator has described the UK education and health sectors as *"ripe for liberalisation"*.'

See the Green Party of England and Wales website at http://
www.greenparty.org.uk/homepage/news/2000/11/igcthreat.htm for evidence
that EU 'neutrality' over public ownership is less than convincing.

The international trade union federation Public Service International
produces critical analyses of EU proposals, including those bearing on competition policy, state aids, and the provision of essential services. Its website
at http://www.world-psi.org/.

Finally, an interesting and unusual study is Poul Thøis Madsen, *Is Culture a
Major Barrier to a Single European Market? The Case of Public Purchasing,*
http://www.i4.auc.dk/pmadsen/purchase.htm.

10   EXTERNAL ECONOMIC RELATIONS

Books

Amnesty International, *Global Trade, Labour and Human Rights* (AI, 2000).
European Commission, *Towards a More Coherent Global Economic Order* (Kogan
    Page, 1998).
Nikolas V. Gianaris, *The North American Free Trade Agreement and the European
    Union* (Praeger, 1998).
Klaus Heindensohn, *Europe and World Trade* (Pinter, 1995).
Marjorie Lister (ed.), *European Union Development Policy* (St Martin's Press,
    1998).
Carolyn Rhodes (ed.), *The European Union in the World Community* (Lynne
    Rienner, 1998).

Websites, Papers, etc.

The European Parliament has produced two *Fact Sheets* on world trade. They
can be accessed at http://www.europarl.eu.int/factsheets/default_en.htm.

One of the best sources of general background reading on trade-related issues
and other aspects of international political economy is the website *Global
Issues That Affect Everyone* at http://www.globalissues.org/index.html.

For an example of the EU's trade with one important part of the world, see
the unattributed article, *The Evolution of Trade Between Latin America and the
European Union* on the University of Texas website at http://
lanic.utexas.edu/project/sela/eng_docs/intevol.htm.

Women In Development Europe (WIDE) produced a briefing for the first
WTO ministerial in December, 1996 entitled *A Gender Perspective on European
Union Trade Policies with Case Studies of the Philippines and Vietnam,* posted at
http://www.eurosur.org/wide/genderpe.htm.

The UK government *National Statistics Theme 6: External Trade: External and Intra-European Trade* 'offers a textual summary of the latest figures on external trade by the member states by country and by product group. It also features trade by the main non-EU countries.' You will have to register to use it. The URL is http://datashop.dur.ac.uk/moby/theme/theme6/intraextra/.

An example of a critique of EU development policy is provided by development NGOCIDSE at http://www.cidse.org/pubs/euafpt2.htm : *Towards True Partnership: EU–Africa Summit, A CIDSE Position Paper: European Union Development Policy* (2000).

A more general critique, from Oxfam UK, entitled *The European Union: A Potential Global Force for Change*, is at http://www.oxfam.org.uk/policy/papers/eu2.htm.

11 EMPLOYMENT AND SOCIAL POLICY

Books

Matti Alestalo and Pekka Kosonen (eds), *Welfare Systems and European Integration: Proceedings from COST A7 Workshop in Tampere, Finland, 24–27 August 1995* (University of Tampere, 1995).
Gerda Falkner, *EU Social Policy in the 1990s: Towards a Corporatist Policy Community* (Routledge, 1998).
Linda Hantrais, *Social Policy in the European Union* (St Martin's Press, 1995).
Stephen Leibfried and Paul Pierson (eds), *European Social Policy : Between Fragmentation and Integration* (Brookings Institute, 1995).
Tamara Routledge, *European Social Law and Policy* (Longman, 1998).
Valerie Symes, *Unemployment and Employment Policy in the European Union* (Kogan Page, 1998).

Websites, Papers, etc.

Kevin Chernosky, *European Union Social Protocol* at http://www.pitt.edu/~heinisch/eu_integ3.html.

Kevin Chernovsky, *European Integration and the Welfare State: European Union Specific Programs and Regional Development*, http://www.pitt.edu/~heinisch/eu_integ4.html. A list of EU industrial relations measures, with links to full texts, is at http://europa.eu.int/eur-lex/en/lif/reg/en_register_05202030.html.

Shirley Hixson, *Democracy, Sovereignty and Popular Choice in the European Union Social Dialogue: Is it Democratic or Simply the Tyranny of Experts? How Can it be Justified?* at http://www.pitt.edu/~heinisch/eu_integ5.html , and *The Effects of Monetary Union on National Social Policies* at http://www.pitt.edu/~heinisch/eu_integ8.html.

Fritz W. Scharpf, 'Economic Integration, Democracy and the Welfare State', *Journal of European Public Policy* 4:1, March 1997 pp. 18–36.

Ignazio Visco, 'Labour market performance and the OECD jobs strategy', *OECD Economic Outlook*, June, 1998.

Rhianon Visinsky, *European Social Policy from 'Rome' to 'Maastricht'*, http://www.pitt.edu/~heinisch/eu_integ2.html.

Malcolm Wicks, 'Beware the monetarist resurgence', *New Statesman*, 28 August 1998.

(No author given) *European Integration and the Welfare State* at *http://www.pitt.edu/~heinisch/eu_integ1.html*.

12   THE ENVIRONMENT

Books

Susan Baker, Maria Kousis and Dick Richardson, *The Politics of Sustainable Development: Theory, Policy and Practice within the European Union* (Routledge, 1997).
Pamela M. Barnes and Ian G. Barnes, *Environmental Policy in the European Union* (Routledge, June 1998).
Wyn Grant, Duncan Matthews and Peter Newell, *The Effectiveness of European Union Environmental Policy* (Palgrave, 2000).
Christopher Knill and Andrea Lenschow, *Implementing European Union Environmental Policy: New Directions and Old Problems* (Manchester University Press, 2000).
David Pinder (ed.), *The New Europe: Economy, Society and Environment* (John Wiley & Son, 1998).
Clive Potter (ed.), *Against the Grain: Agri-Environmental Reform in the United States and European Union* (CABI, 1998).
David Malin Roodman, *Paying the Piper: Subsidies, Politics, and the Environment* (Worldwatch Institute, 1996).

Websites, Papers, etc.

About.com's *Europe and the Environment* site gives a great deal of straightforward information at http://environment.about.com/newsissues/environment/library/weekly/bleur.htm.

The official European Environment Agency can be found at http://www.eea.eu.int/. Not to be confused with the European Environment Bureau, which represents NGOs and is at http://www.eeb.org.

The European Commission's Directorate General for Environment's site is at http://europa.eu.int/comm/dgs/environment/index_en.htm.

A more succinct propaganda source is the EU site at http://www.greeneurope.org/.

An official Commission site with links to other EU information sources on such matters as integrated coastal zone management, and climate change, is at http://www.eur-focalpt.org/links-eu.htm.

The European Union in the US website also has links to useful information through its environment page at http://www.eurunion.org/legislat/envirweb.htm.

The European Parliament Environment Committee can be found at http://www.europarl.eu.int/comparl/envi/default_en.htm.

A good brief summary of EU decision-making procedures and bodies is included in The Fridtjof Nansen Institute, *Yearbook of International Co-operation on Environment and Development, 1999–2000* at http://www.ngo.grida.no/ggynet/igo/eu/htm.

Friends of the Earth Europe produces critical comments on EU environmental initiatives and is at http://www.foeeurope.org/.

13   THE COMMON AGRICULTURAL POLICY AND COMMON FISHERIES POLICY

Books

European Commission, *Towards a Common Agricultural and Rural Policy for Europe* (Office for the Official Publications of the European Communities,1997).
Rosemary Fennell, *The Common Agricultural Policy: Continuity and Change* (Clarendon Press, 1997).
Wyn Grant, *The Common Agricultural Policy* (Palgrave, 1997).
Mike Holden and David Garrod, *The Common Fisheries Policy* (Blackwell Science, 1996).
Adrian Kay, *The Reform of the Common Agricultural Policy: The Case of the MacSharry Reforms* (CABI, 1998).
Ronan J. Long and Peter A. Curran, *Enforcing the Common Fisheries Policy* (Fishing News Books, 1998).
Deborah J. Pain *et al.*, *Farming and Birds in Europe: The Common Agricultural Policy and Its Implications for Bird Conservation* (Academic Press, 1997).
Christopher Ritson and David Harvey, *The Common Agricultural Policy* (2nd edn, Oxford UP, 1997).

Websites, Papers, etc.

The Commission Directorate General for Agriculture website is at http://europa.eu.int/comm/dg06/index.htm or you can go straight to Agenda 2000, http://europa.eu.int/comm/dg06/ag2000/index_en.htm.

A lively page of news about and criticism of the CAP is *Wyn Grant's Common Agricultural Policy Page* at http://members.tripod.com/~WynGrant/Wyn-GrantCAPpage.html.

Richard Howarth, *Global Britain Briefing Note No. 3: The Failures of CAP* at http://www.keele.ac.uk/socs/ks40/capref.

The US National Center for Policy Analysis has a brief look at why the CAP is 'disastrous' at http://www.ncpa.org/pi/internat/pd081000e.html.

International Institute for Sustainable Development, *The Reform of the European Union Common Agricultural Policy*, http://iisd1.iisd.ca/greenbud/reform.htm.

How Does the CAP Work?, http://bized.ac.uk/compfact/mlc/mlc44.htm.

Royal Society for the Protection of Birds (RSPB), *Farming and Wildlife*, http://www.rspb.org.uk/wildlife/frame.asp.

Consumers in Europe Group (CEG), *The Common Agricultural Policy and Consumers*, http://www.ceg.co.uk/cap.htm.htm.

Netherlands Ministry of Agriculture, *The Common Agricultural Policy in the Future: Discussion Paper*, http://www.minlnv.nl/international/policy/inta/notutie.htm.

The Scottish Office Department of Agriculture, Environment and Fisheries, *The Common Agricultural Policy Factsheet*, http://www.scotland.gov.uk/agri/documents/capf-00.htm.

The website of the EU Community Initiative on rural development, LEADER, is at http://www.rural-europe.aeidl.be/. If you're not sure what a Community Initiative is, go to the chapters on social policy (11) and regional policy (15).

There is a 'euro-sceptic' website on the CAP at http://www.kc3.co.uk/~dt/farm.htm.

The European Commission Fisheries Directorate General is at http://europa.eu.int/comm/dgs/fisheries/index_en.htm.

The European Commission Fisheries Directorate General, *European Union Aid for the Development of the Fishing Industry in the United Kingdom (1994–99)*, http://europa.eu.int/comm/dgs/fisheries/index_en.htm.

The Commission also produces a magazine, *Fisheries*, available on line at http://europa.eu.int/comm/fisheries/doc_et_publ/magaz/fishing_en.htm.

Roger Bate *The Common Fisheries Policy: A Sinking Ship*, originally published in the *Wall Street Journal* during June, 2000 (the website gives no precise date) is at http://www.environmentprobe.org/enviroprobe/evpress/0700_wsj.html.

Easily the most entertaining and one of the most informative of websites on the CFP is the Fleetwood Trawlermen's site at http://www.fleetwood-trawlers.fsnet.co.uk/euro.html It includes a splendid piece entitled *European Lunatics Ruin Our Industry*, is progressive and internationalist in its perspective, and should be read by anyone who wants to know why the EU and its Commission are not the most loved institutions in the UK and many other member states.

14   TRANSPORT

Books

Stijn Vanhandsaeme *et al.* (eds), *Lost in Concrete: Activist Guide to European Transport Policies* (A SEED Europe, 1996).
John Whitelegg, *Transport for a Sustainable Future: the Case of Europe* (Belhaven Press, 1993).
John Whitelegg, *Critical Mass: Transport, Environment and Society in the Twenty-first Century* (Pluto Press, 1997).
Winfried Wolf, *Car Mania: A Critical History of Transport* (Pluto Press, 1996).

Websites, Papers, etc.

Go to http://europa.eu.int/comm/transport/site_map_en.html to navigate around the whole of Directorate General Transport's site.

A collection of official EU publications can be found at the site of the Cordis (Research into Sustainable Mobility) website at http://www.cordis.lu/transport/src/public1.htm. They include:

The Citizens' Network: Fulfilling the Potential of Public Passenger Transport in Europe: European Commission Green Paper.

Towards a New Maritime Strategy: Communication from the Commission to the Council, the European Parliament, the Economic and Social Committee and the Committee of the Regions Towards Fair and Efficient Pricing in Transport: Policy Options for Internalising the External Costs of Transport in the European Union.

The Common Transport Policy Action Programme 1995–2000: Communication to the Council, the European Parliament, the Economic and Social Committee and the Committee of Regions.

White Paper on Revitalising the Community's Railways Communication on Intermodal Freight Transport Communication on Road Transport Telematics in Europe.

European Commission Transport and Cohesion, http:// www.inforegio. cec.eu.int/wbdoc/docoffic/communic/cotrans/home_en.htm.

Detailed statistical data on transport in Europe is available at the Commission's site at http://europa.eu.int/comm/transport/tif/index.htm.

Sytze A. Rienstra *et al.*, 'Assessing the complementarity of common transport policy objectives: a scenario approach' can be downloaded from http://ideas.uqam.ca/ideas/data/Papers/dgrvuarem1997–70.html.

International Labour Organisation, *Symposium on the Social and Labour Consequences of Technological Developments, Deregulation and Privatization of Transport: Background Document* (ILO, 1999) is at http://www.ilo.org/ public/english/dialogue/sector/techmeet/sdpt99/sdptr.htm.

The WWW Virtual Library provides links to official and unofficial EU transport policy websites, as well as a bibliography. URL: http:// www.pitt.edu/~wwwes/transport.guide.html.

European Cyclists' Federation comments on the *Commission Communication on the Common Transport Policy: Sustainable Mobility: Perspectives for the Future* are at http://www.ecf.com/html/newpubl.html.

A European Information Service summary of the 1998 White Paper on TENS is at http://www.findarticles.com/cf_0/m0WXI/2355/53180463/p1/ article. jhtml. The UK government's response to the White Paper is at http:// www.detr.gov.uk/itwp/ctp/.

A speech given by Transport Commissioner Neil Kinnock to the French National Assembly (Parliament) in December, 1998, is at http:// europa.eu.int/comm/transport/global/speeches/speech98289.html.

Gerd Wartenberg, *Opinion of the Committee of the Regions on the Pan-European Dimension of Transport Policy* (Committee of the Regions, 1997).

European Report 26 July 2000 'EU Enlargement: 14 more transport and environment projects approved for ISPA' available on line at http:// www.findarticles.com/m0WXI/2000_July_26/63698306/p1/article.jhtml.

A good bibliography on 'European Transport', with links is on a Nottingham University website at http://www.nottingham.ac.uk/sbe/planbiblios/bibs/ sustrav/refs/ST36.html.

A succinct anti-TENs case is made at http://www.scotweb.co.uk/environ-ment/climate/tens/index.html.

An interesting story from European Information Service (EIS) (26 April 2000) in which the Commission reiterates its concerns regarding the balance between road and rail, http://www.findarticles.com/cf_0/m0WXI/2000_April_19/61579923/p1/article.jhtml.

Another, also from EIS (6 June1998) on the 'pan-European' dimension is at http://www.findarticles.com/cf_0/m0WXI/1998_June_6/50059652/p1/article.jhtml. while Transport Commissioner Loyola de Palacio gives her views on sustainable development in EIS (7 June 2000) at http://www.findarticles.com/cf_0/m0WXI/2000_June_7/62558232/p1/article.jhtml.

And some critical pamphlets not, as far as I know, available on line:

François Meienberg and Matthiaas Schickhofer, *Missing Greenlinks: Examination of the Commission's Guidelines for a Decision about the Trans-European Networks and Proposal for Ecological Restructuring* (Greenpeace Switzerland, 1995).

Olivia Bina *et al.*, *The Impact of Trans-European Networks on Nature Conservation: A Pilot Project* (Bird Life International, 1995).

15   REGIONAL POLICY

Books

Ash Amin and John Tomaney (eds), *Behind the Myth of European Union: Prospects for Cohesion* (Routledge, 1995).
John Bactler and Ivan Turok *The Coherence of EU Regional Policy: Contrasting Perspectives on the Structural Funds* (Jessica Kingsley, 1998).
Kenneth John Button and Eric J. Pentecost, *Regional Economic Performance Within the European Union* (Edward Elgar, 1999).
Jeffrey Harrop, *Structural Funding and Employment in the European Union: Financing the Path to Integration* (Edward Elgar, 1996).
Reiner Martin, *The Regional Dimension in European Public Policy: Convergence or Divergence?* (St Martin's Press, 1999).
Morris L. Sweet, *Regional Economic Development in the European Union and North America* (Praeger, 1999).

Websites, Papers, etc.

Kaisa Paavilainen *Regional Policy of the European Union,* http://www.helsinki.fi/~kepaavil/.

'Structural funds: new users' guide published' *European Report*, 6 February 1999, http://www.findarticles.com/cf_0/m0WXI/1999_Feb_6/53733273/ p1/article.jhtml?term=european+union+regional+cohesion.

16   INDUSTRIAL POLICY AND ENERGY

Books

Thomas C. Lawton, *European Industrial Policy and Competitiveness: Concepts and Instruments* (St Martin's Press, 1998).
Wolf Sauter, *Competition Law and Industrial Policy in the EU* (Oxford UP, 1998).
Collier Ute, *Energy and Environment in the European Union: The Challenge of Integration* (Avebury, 1995). NB a new edition of this book is planned, but was unavailable at the time of writing.

Websites, Papers, etc.

The website of the European Commission Directorate General for Energy is at http://europa.eu.int/comm/dgs/energy_transport/index_en.html.

As well as the website of the Directorate General for Research at http://europa.eu.int/comm/dgs/research/index_en.html, the Joint Research Centre maintains its own site, http://www.jrc.cec.eu.int/index.asp.

The most valuable site for research information, however, is the Community Research and Development Information Service (CORDIS) at http://www.cordis.lu/en/home.html.

The list of on-line sources headed 'European Union: competition, industrial and enterprise policy' at http://www.pitt.edu/~wwwes/competition.guide.html is comprehensive.

Index

Compiled by Sue Carlton

IMF (International Monetary Fund)
138, 143
immigration 11, 12, 39, 56, 57
see also inward migration
imports
dumping 84
external trade 83–5
and fair trade 69–70
from former colonies 84, 87
restrictions on 84–5
surveillance 84
trade embargoes 84, 85
industrial policy 8, 12, 128–33
information technology 77, 133
infrastructure
and environmental damage 104
improving 77
investment in 124, 129
road-building 104–5, 116, 119,
120
transport 116, 120, 125
institutions
reforms 3, 9
relationships between 6
Instrument for Structural Policies
for Pre-Accession Aid (ISPA)
40, 41
integration
and economic and monetary
union 122
and Nice Treaty 6, 12, 28
integrationism 3–5, 18, 20, 22, 36,
134, 135, 143
Intergovernmental Conferences
(IGCs) 17, 44
internal market *see* Single European
Market (SEM)
international agreements 11, 85, 87
International Monetary Fund (IMF)
138, 143
inward migration 10–11, 37, 39,
74–6
Iraq 85
Ireland 46, 66, 121, 122, 125
Israel 30
Italy 18, 62, 66

jobs, protection of 73, 124
Joint Research Centre (JRC) 132

Jordan 87
judicial co-operation 56
Justice and Home Affairs (JHA) 4–5,
8, 56–8, 140

Kohl, Helmut 60
Kok, Wim 92
Kosovo 46, 48
Kurdestan 43

labour markets
direct intervention 93
free movement 4, 74–7, 80,
89–90
labour mobility 61
reform of 59–60
see also employment; unemployment
Latvia 41
laws 26–8
legislative procedures 29
role of institutions 27
treaty base 27
lead 108
Leader (Community Initiative for
poorer regions) 126
Lebanon 87
Leonardo (EU training and
education programme) 101
Lichtenstein 79
LIFE (EU fund for nature conservation projects) 41
Lingua (EU language education
programme) 101
Lisbon Summit (1999) 89, 94
Lithuania 41
Lomé Convention 87, 111
Luxembourg 62, 66
Luxembourg Summit (1998) 94

Maastricht Treaty (Treaty on
European Union) 3–5, 7–8
and citizenship 51
and co-decision 22
and Common Foreign and
Security Policy 48
and convergence criteria 60
and development policy 88
education and training 101